T0286813

Cambridge Elements ≡

Elements in Applied Evolutionary Science
edited by
David F. Bjorklund
Florida Atlantic University

AN INTRODUCTION TO POSITIVE EVOLUTIONARY PSYCHOLOGY

Glenn Geher
SUNY New Paltz

Megan Fritche
SUNY New Paltz

Avrey Goodwine
SUNY New Paltz

Julia Lombard
SUNY New Paltz

Kaitlyn Longo
SUNY New Paltz

Darcy Montana
SUNY New Paltz

THE EVOLUTION INSTITUTE

CAMBRIDGE
UNIVERSITY PRESS

CAMBRIDGE
UNIVERSITY PRESS

Shaftesbury Road, Cambridge CB2 8EA, United Kingdom

One Liberty Plaza, 20th Floor, New York, NY 10006, USA

477 Williamstown Road, Port Melbourne, VIC 3207, Australia

314–321, 3rd Floor, Plot 3, Splendor Forum, Jasola District Centre,
New Delhi – 110025, India

103 Penang Road, #05–06/07, Visioncrest Commercial, Singapore 238467

Cambridge University Press is part of Cambridge University Press & Assessment,
a department of the University of Cambridge.

We share the University's mission to contribute to society through the pursuit of
education, learning and research at the highest international levels of excellence.

www.cambridge.org
Information on this title: www.cambridge.org/9781009286855

DOI: 10.1017/9781009286817

First published 2023

A catalogue record for this publication is available from the British Library.

ISBN 978-1-009-28685-5 Paperback
ISSN 2752-9428 (online)
ISSN 2752-941X (print)

An Introduction to Positive Evolutionary Psychology

Elements in Applied Evolutionary Science

DOI: 10.1017/9781009286817
First published online: April 2023

Glenn Geher
SUNY New Paltz

Megan Fritche
SUNY New Paltz

Avrey Goodwine
SUNY New Paltz

Julia Lombard
SUNY New Paltz

Kaitlyn Longo
SUNY New Paltz

Darcy Montana
SUNY New Paltz

Author for correspondence: Glenn Geher, geherg@newpaltz.edu

Abstract: Over the past few decades, evolutionary psychology has shed light on such features of the human experience as mating, love, religion, aggression, warfare, physical health, mental health, and more. The field of positive psychology has progressed along a parallel trajectory, using behavioral science techniques to help our understanding of human thriving at the individual and community levels. This Element is dedicated to the integration of positive and evolutionary psychology, with an eye toward using Darwinian-inspired concepts to help advance our understanding of human thriving. The Element describes the basic ideas of this new approach to behavioral science as well as examples that dip into various aspects of the human experience, including such topics as health, education, friendships, love, and more – all with an eye toward providing a roadmap for the application of Darwinian principles to better understand human thriving and the good life.

Keywords: evolutionary psychology, positive psychology, positive evolutionary psychology, Charles Darwin, evolutionary mismatch

ISBNs: 9781009286855 (PB), 9781009286817 (OC)
ISSNs: 2752-9428 (online), 2752-941X (print)

Contents

1 What Is Positive Evolutionary Psychology?

When Charles Darwin (1859) so famously explained to the world that the entirety of life on earth, including humans, is largely the result of natural selection, our shared understanding of who we are shifted both qualitatively and permanently. And when he famously applied the evolutionary principles that he had discovered to the domain of behavior (e.g., Darwin, 1872), he rocked our understanding of the world and of our place in it even more so. For all intents and purposes, Darwin himself started the field of evolutionary psychology, showing us how to apply evolutionary principles to give us insights into behavioral and concomitant psychological processes. When people talk about when the field of evolutionary psychology started, to our minds, the answer clearly goes back to Darwin.

Scores later, when renowned behavioral scientist Martin Seligman (see Seligman & Csikszentmihalyi, 2000) suggested that the behavioral sciences change from a focus on problematic features of the human experience (e.g., disorders of mental health) to a focus on the positive aspects of the human experience, including such outcomes as happiness and growth, the field of positive psychology was famously born, leading to a global and ongoing effort to scientifically understand factors associated with human thriving at both the individual and community levels. As we describe throughout this Element, this large-scale initiative has led to a landslide of scholarship and insight into the human condition.

With our recent book, *Positive Evolutionary Psychology: Darwin's Guide to Living a Richer Life*, we (Geher & Wedberg, 2020) worked to integrate the ideas of these fields into a coherent and organized effort to shed light on the positives of the human experience via the application of Darwinian principles. As we addressed in detail in that work, past scholarship in the field of evolutionary psychology has all but fully neglected the positive psychology movement – and vice versa. Systematic examinations of literature cited in positive psychology journals, for instance, rarely touch on work conducted in the evolutionary behavioral sciences (see Geher & Wedberg, 2020). Similarly, systematic examinations of work couched as *positive psychology* virtually never draws on literature from the evolutionary behavioral sciences. These two significant and growing areas of scholarship on the human condition basically have been progressing for decades now without being informed by the other whatsoever.

The field of *positive evolutionary psychology* is designed to change all that. Given the ubiquitous and powerful capacity for evolutionary psychology to inform all areas of the behavioral sciences (see Carmen et al., 2013), we believe that using an evolutionary approach to address questions of positive psychology has enormous untapped potential to help us best understand the science of living the good life.

To understand the nature of positive evolutionary psychology – the focus of this Element – we need to understand the basics of its two primary components: evolutionary psychology and positive psychology. Evolutionary psychology (see Buss, 2019; Geher, 2014) is an approach to understanding human behavior by seeing human behavior as a product of deep evolutionary forces, such as natural selection. While all evolutionary principles that have been discovered by Darwin and his intellectual disciples (e.g., Trivers, 1972) are fair game in the work of evolutionary psychology, a large focus is found in work that sees behavioral patterns as adaptations that follow from natural selection-based reasoning.

A classic example is found in the very basic human fear of snakes (see Öhman & Mineka, 2001). Fear of snakes represents one of the most common human fears, worldwide. And this fact makes good sense given that all humans have their roots in sub-Saharan Africa, where venomous snakes are common. Under such conditions, which characterized our ancestral contexts (known as the Environment of Evolutionary Adaptedness or EEA; Bowlby, 1969), individuals who tended to naturally have a fear of snakes were more likely than others to survive and thus, to reproduce. That is because those who did not fear snakes were more likely to find themselves as victims of fatally poisonous snakebites and, accordingly, die Darwinian deaths, failing to both survive and reproduce. To the extent that fear of snakes is a heritable element of human psychology (as so many features of our psychology are; see Miller, 2000), we can easily see how fear of snakes, a basic and straightforward psychological attribute, can be understood in evolutionary terms.

Compared with evolutionary psychology, the field of positive psychology tends to be much more applied by its very nature. Positive psychology (see Peterson, 2013), which has its roots in the humanistic psychology movement that started in the middle of the twentieth century (c.f., Bugental, 1964), has a goal that is beyond simply better understanding the human condition. Positive psychology, based on its very nature, is all about using behavioral science to help us make improvements in human functioning at the individual and community levels. A basic idea here is that all humans are capable of thriving – of living up to their potential – of experiencing such positive affective states as happiness and self-love – and of taking steps to build positive and enriching communities that benefit individuals as well as broader groups of individuals. Using a diverse array of scientific methodologies (see McMahan & Estes, 2015), positive psychologists are all about developing ways to improve the human condition.

In short, positive evolutionary psychology is merging of these two fields. The basic idea here, elaborated in detail across this Element, is to address issues that have typically been within the purview of positive psychology, such as factors that cultivate happiness, via the application of principles and research findings from the evolutionary behavioral sciences. Positive evolutionary psychology is a field dedicated to using Darwin's big ideas to shed light on the positives of the human lived experience. See Figure 1 for visual representation of the relationship between the field of positive and evolutionary psychology across time.

Coming from a slightly different background and perspective, renowned evolutionary biologist David Sloan Wilson (2019, 2011) has written extensively about how evolutionary principles can shed light on all kinds of human outcomes, at both the individual and group levels. Drawing largely on this model of multilevel selection, Wilson (2019) focuses on how our evolved nature includes a combination of (a) selfish attributes (which arose, per Wilson's terminology,

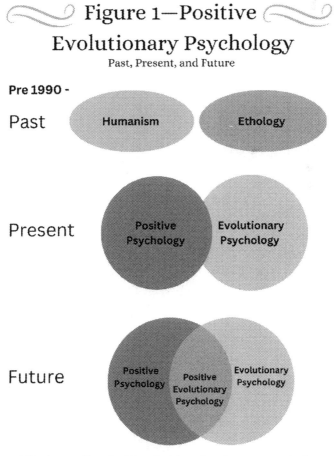

Figure 1—Positive Evolutionary Psychology
Past, Present, and Future

Pre 1990 -

Past Humanism Ethology

Present Positive Psychology Evolutionary Psychology

Future Positive Psychology Positive Evolutionary Psychology Evolutionary Psychology

Figure 1 Understanding the historical interface between evolutionary and positive psychology

via *within-group selection* pressures) and (b) other-oriented attributes, including prosocial behavior (which arose, per Wilson's terminology, via *between-group selection* pressures). In presenting our evolved behavior in this way, Wilson provides models of how evolutionary principles and scholarship have helped to shape all kinds of positive human outcomes, such as improvements in social functioning among adolescents (Wilson, 2011), productivity and happiness in organizational functioning, efforts to increase sustainability in terms of environmental issues (Wilson, 2019), and more.

Other work by such academic pugilists as Steven Pinker (2012) The Better Angels of Our Nature: Why Violence Has Declined. Penguin. draws largely on evolutionary principles to help shed light on large-scale, societal issues such as levels of violence, malnutrition, and violence on a global scale. Using an empirically based approach, on this point, Pinker argues that modern industrialized societies, while highly imperfect for various reasons, actually have proven successful in reducing rates of such adverse phenomena as warfare and violence.

In many ways, these scholars have paved the way for the emergence of positive evolutionary psychology as a discrete academic field of inquiry that draws on a vast literature in the evolutionary behavioral sciences to help facilitate human growth and positive change at both the individual and community levels.

In citing much of the most recent published research that integrates evolutionary and positive psychology, this Element is organized to help the reader understand the field of positive evolutionary psychology from multiple angles. Sections in the Element are organized as follows:

- Why Do We Need Positive Evolutionary Psychology?
- Evolutionary Mismatch as a Foundational Concept in Positive Evolutionary Psychology
- Understanding Family through an Evolutionary Lens
- Evolutionary Psychology Applied to Education
- Evolutionary Psychology, Happiness, and Mental Health
- Evolutionary Psychology and the Cultivation of Community
- The Evolution of Social and Moral Emotions
- Evolutionary Psychology and Physical Health
- Future Directions in Positive Evolutionary Psychology

Welcome to the new field of positive evolutionary psychology.

2 Why Do We Need Positive Evolutionary Psychology?

As defined in the previous section, positive evolutionary psychology is an emerging area in the field of psychology with basic principles from the marriage of positive and evolutionary psychology. Although the field is new and still being developed, it integrates critical bodies of literature to help advance our understanding and potential improvement of the human experience. By taking the core principles from two powerful fields of psychology, with the goal of *thriving better*, the field of positive evolutionary psychology stands to become a powerful approach of psychology, essential for human improvement.

The field of evolutionary psychology seeks to understand why patterns of behavior and psychological processes exist through the lens of Darwinian principles, allowing for a new understanding of what it means to be human. On the other hand, positive psychology seeks to expand our understanding of the positive aspects of human existence. Both fields independently exhibit the power to expand our knowledge and improve the human experience, but the framework outlined by the marriage of the two is something that we believe is an integral part of the development of psychology as a discipline.

Similar to the academic fields it is derived from, positive evolutionary psychology gives insight into a broad range of topics – as outlined by Geher and Wedberg (2020) – including politics, religion, love, social relationships, resilience, and an evolutionary perspective on taking a positive approach to life. And more. Positive evolutionary psychology seeks to advance our understanding of positive aspects of the human experience such as these, and in doing so it furthers our understanding of ways to improve the human experience. For example, positive evolutionary psychology can be used to increase positive feelings and behaviors in the long-term manner through *positive psychological intervention* (PPI), which have traditionally been fully under the purview of positive psychology (Schueller & Parks, 2014). The goal of a PPI is extremely similar to the core contents of this field, and effective PPIs have been shown to lead to decreases in depression symptoms as well as increases in overall well-being (Boiler et al., 2013; Sin & Lyubomirsky, 2009). Studies on PPIs have found that they can lead to improved functioning across various environments (Sergeant & Mongrain, 2015) for people of all ages (Leontopoulou, 2015). Positive psychology-based approaches serve to benefit people of all ages in all aspects of life.

Positive evolutionary psychology also potentially serves as an important bridge between evolutionary psychology and other areas of academic psychology. Historically, evolutionary psychology has not been well received throughout the academic world (see Geher & Gambacorta, 2010), despite its countless contributions to the understanding of human behavior. Marrying the concepts and ideas of evolutionary psychology with positive psychology presents them as a "kinder, gentler evolutionary psychology" (Geher & Wedberg, 2020, p. 23). The evolutionary perspective has shown an unparalleled capacity to expand our understanding of human behavior through the generation of new research questions, and, in turn, new research findings. The resistance that has often been launched at the field is, to our minds, depriving scholars of the insights it can provide and the understanding of human behavior that it can provide. By developing the field of positive evolutionary psychology, an area of study is being developed in which scholars can take the tools from the evolutionary perspective and apply them to research questions that search to improve the lives of human beings without (in theory) poorly construed perceptions of the field of evolutionary psychology getting in the way.

The field of positive evolutionary psychology is still new, but it is clear that it is an inherently important field to further understand and improve the human experience. With goals that seek to improve the positive aspects of the human experience, this field is integral to the development of the field of psychology and to the improvement of the human experience.

3 Evolutionary Mismatch as a Foundational Concept in Positive Evolutionary Psychology

Evolutionary mismatch (see Geher, 2014) exists when an organism is currently living in an environment that is mismatched from the ancestral environment that surrounded the evolutionary history of its ancestors. Despite the vast arrays of technologies we have developed at a global level, we face the same challenges and problems dealt with by our ancestors. Some may say that we are actually less equipped to face these challenges now that we have such advanced technologies at our everyday disposal. Douglas Kenrick and David Lundberg-Kenrick outlined multiple examples in their new book *Solving Modern Problems with a Stone-Age Brain* (2022). For example, one of the commonly mentioned hurdles in evolutionary psychology is partner infidelity. In ancestral conditions it was much more difficult to be disloyal to your partner as a part of such a small community where you know everyone and everyone knows you (vis-à-vis Dunbar's number (1992), elaborated on later in this section). In our current world, one can walk into a busy restaurant without knowing a single person. Life is much more anonymous in the exponentially larger societies we are living in today. Because of this, it is much easier for someone to be unfaithful and get away with it. Another example of mismatch can be seen in our physical proximity to those with whom we are closely linked. In ancestral conditions, you were in close proximity to everyone you were linked to. In the current environment, family and friend groups are scattered all around the world due to work, schooling, and so on. This distance is decreasing the likelihood that we will join social groups or have social gatherings with friends. Not having these close social connections increases mortality as much as smoking fifteen cigarettes a day (Kenrick & Lundberg-Kenrick, 2022).

One of the goals of positive evolutionary psychology is to use the knowledge we have about our evolution and human sociality to benefit our present-day lives. By viewing the implications of the evolutionary mismatches we have in our society, we can advance the goals of positive evolutionary psychology by understanding problems of the human experience that result from modern contexts being out of line with ancestral conditions. The concept of mismatch has been raised in many different disciplines such as biology (e.g., Schlaepfer et al., 2002), economics (Burnham, 2016; Kanazawa, 2004), health (Buss, 2000), medicine (Nesse & Williams, 1995), and ecological conservation (Li et al., 2018), as well as multiple psychological disciplines such as social (Maner & Kenrick, 2010), cognitive (Tooby & Cosmides, 1990), developmental (Bjorklund, 2021), and organizational (Spranger et al., 2012; van Vugt & Ronay, 2014) psychologies. As societies continue to globalize and human-induced changes continue to alter our environment, evolutionary mismatch is becoming increasingly prevalent and relevant.

As mismatch often comes with consequences that negatively affect psychological and physical health, it is important not only for psychological research but also for achieving a better understanding of the modern world in order to address the numerous problems we face (Li et al., 2018). Thus, the idea of mismatch is critical to the broader concept of positive evolutionary psychology.

3.1 Dunbar's Number and Society

In evolutionary psychology one of the most important figures to keep in mind is known as *Dunbar's number* (Dunbar, 1992). Dunbar's number is the idea that the nomadic clans our ancestors lived in rarely exceed a population of 150. The clans consisted mostly of kin and those you had known your entire life (see Geher & Wedberg, 2020). Encountering strangers was a rarity and would often be viewed as something dangerous, which explains the reason why today we may become nervous or anxiety-ridden when having to confront large groups of strangers or peers.

Modern, westernized societies tend to be comprised of communities that are off-the-scale when it comes to Dunbar's number. For instance, if we look at major cities like New York City, we see populations in the millions. Even modern "small towns" (e.g., New Paltz, NY, with a population of about 10,000 people) have populations that often are wildly off the charts when it comes to Dunbar's number. Thus, modern community sizes are highly mismatched from the kinds of communities that our ancestors evolved within.

This mismatch leads to higher crime rates and increased prevalence of mental health issues when compared to small communities (Figueredo et al., 2006; Srivastava, 2009). The fact that there are more social and crime-related issues, per capita, in larger cities around the world speaks strongly to the adverse effects of evolutionary mismatch when it comes to group size.

3.2 Large-Scale Implications of Modern Politics

Dunbar's number also explains why large-scale politics are often so problematic. When we hear stories of humanitarian crises across the world, we may feel angered or emotional over the action, yet our reactions are fleeting (Geher et al., 2015). However, if our communities began restricting our own particular rights, our reactions would be monumental and long-lasting. This difference may be due to the fact that our neocortex can only register information that pertains to relatively small-scale social living and, as such, large-scale political issues are inherently difficult for us to process (Geher & Wedberg, 2020). Modern-day humans are adapted for local and small-scale politics, as we physically and mentally cannot comprehend larger-scale politics. These implications may explain why there is typically such a low voter turnout in the United States (Geher & Wedberg, 2020). If political issues are too complex or individuals do not feel as if the results will personally affect them, the motivation to vote would decrease (Geher & Wedberg, 2020).

Not only does our evolutionary development affect how we view large-scale politics but it also has some sway over how we vote for electoral candidates based on the level of prestige versus dominance one may have. We have evolved to view prestige as having a position of power in an individual's mind, yet this trait is not fear-driven (Henrich & Gil-White, 2001). Instead, it is viewed as an influence over others. An individual with prestige has opinions heavily credited to the standing of the general public (Henrich & Gil-White, 2001). When we look for electoral candidates to vote into office, we are looking for someone with the social and cultural skills needed to lead and create decisions. Often people confuse the difference between prestige and dominance and will make the mistake of believing that a candidate is voted into office because they dominate, but our evolutionary history argues differently.

Based on the foundational evolutionary concept of reproductive success as Darwin's bottom line, evolutionary adaptations all stem from the idea of reproduction, specifically for men, passing their genes onto future generations (Colegrave, 2012). To accomplish this, intrasexual competition often takes place and forces men to adapt to the conditions and terms that women find suitable in a partner; for most women, male parental investment is the leading deciding factor when choosing a long-term partner (Henrich & Gil-White, 2001). Females also typically would select mates with higher social and cultural capacities (Henrich & Gil-White, 2001). As this is the case, females and males tend to prefer partners with more useful survival-related skills (Henrich & Gil-White, 2001). To the extent that these tendencies are at all heritable, these preferences are then passed down to generations through natural selection and become traits we naturally look for in people.

The way this applies to politics and political figures is generally done in the same way we would select a mate, because we evolved to look for these cultural and social skills that are naturally preferred, especially with candidates in our communities. Traits that seem to be highly valued in leaders generally speak to indicators of status, community respect, and high-quality social connections (see Geher & Wedberg, 2020). These are all traits associated with prestige and phenomenon such as dialect changes, which have been shown to map onto ratings of prestige (e.g., with some dialects being evaluated as less prestigious than others; Henrich & Gil-White, 2001).

4 Understanding Family through an Evolutionary Lens

Some of the most fundamental concepts in evolutionary psychology are inclusive fitness (Hamilton, 1964) and kin-selection theory (Eberhard et al., 1975). Inclusive fitness allows us to understand why we are so inclined to help our relatives. According to W. D. Hamilton's theory of inclusive fitness and kin-selection, organisms are more likely to help other conspecifics if they share a higher proportion of their genes. Humans may maximize their own reproductive success in two ways: directly, by mating and having their own offspring, or indirectly, by fostering family members' reproductive success or survival (Ko et al., 2020). Kin-selected altruism indirectly increases our own reproductive success via self-sacrificial behaviors that may promote the survival of relatives who share a proportionate amount of our genes (Eberhard et al., 1975). Additionally, the development of kin-selected altruism may have given rise to other prosocial behaviors engaged outside of the familial-sphere, such as recipro-cal altruism. On average, we are more likely to help our relatives, specifically our children, because they may pass on a high proportion of shared genes.

4.1 Altricial Young, Pair Bonding, and Parental Investment

In comparison to other species, humans have relatively altricial young. Our children are essentially helpless for the first few years of their lives and continue to require a lot of care and support in order to develop and mature into adults.

One reason human children may take longer to mature into adults is due to our brain size and brain complexity. The human female pelvic structure has faced evolutionary pressures to balance the ability to birth infants with larger heads and to maintain the duration of prenatal development and gestation periods (Ruff, 2002). Because the pelvic structure can only withstand so much, infants are born without fully developed brains. Therefore, much of the brain development occurs postnatally, which may require an extended period of time to develop fully (see Flinn et al., 2007). Another reason human children may take more time to develop may be due to the complexity of our social environments. Longer periods of childhood and adolescence may provide us with more time and experience to learn about social contracts, to establish cognitive social abilities, and to develop proficiency in engaging in social interactions (see Flinn et al., 2007).

Effective parenting is required to raise altricial young during these long periods of development to become successful and well-functioning adults. Not only does effective parenting benefit the rearing of a child but it may also contribute to the long-term reproductive success of the parents involved (see Geher et al., 2020). Therefore, humans often invest many resources and time into the rearing of their children (Trivers, 1972). Extensive biparental care, or care from two parents, may increase the efficacy of raising young. Biparental care often requires long-term pair bonds between two individuals (see Flinn et al., 2007). These human pair bonds maximize parental investment and cooperation between partners, thus increasing the potential fitness of children (see Ko et al., 2020).

Interestingly, biparental pair bonds may have been perpetuated further by the cultural evolution of monogamous marriage. Besides the benefits of increased biparental care for offspring, monogamous marriage may also provide benefits in reducing the costs of intrasexual competition. In societies with more intergroup competition, a reduction in intrasexual competition may help to decrease violence, abuse, and crime within groups. In other words, lowering the frequency of intrasexual competition may increase cooperation within groups, allowing for greater group-level fitness. As human societies and cultures continue to rapidly evolve, more social inequalities emerge, which demand greater group cooperation. In some communities, the cultural evolution of monogamous marriage may help to mediate some of these demands and issues, as well as increase parental investment (Henrich et al., 2012).

Compared to any other relative, human mothers generally invest the most in their children (Geary, 2005). For this reason, human parental investment between males and females is often asymmetrical. Females have higher caloric investment in their offspring due to gestation and nursing periods (see Ko et al., 2020). Some events in our evolutionary history may account for this high level of maternal investment. For instance, the emergence of bipedalism may have reduced the size of female pelvic structures, leading to shorter gestation periods. Due to this, humans are essentially born premature and require longer periods of postnatal development (see Pavard et al., 2007). In fact, compared to other species of primates, humans have much lengthier childhoods and periods of adolescence (Flinn et al., 2007; Ko et al., 2020). The altricial nature of human young demands a large amount of parental investment, often from the mother. The growth of human body sizes throughout our evolutionary history may have also necessitated more nutritional support (providing food, initially via breast-feeding) and nurturance (affectionate behaviors and education) from mothers for children to grow into their larger adult bodies (see Pavard et al., 2007). Today, positive parental investment from mothers has been shown to help establish healthy attachment styles, which contribute to children's social development (Flaherty & Sadler, 2011). From an evolutionary perspective, raising children is a costly, yet crucial, endeavor for mothers, often requiring help from other relatives, specifically from fathers and grandmothers (Mace, 2015).

Although there are asymmetries in human parental investment (see Geher, 2014), both male and female parents play important roles in contributing to the success of their offspring. In more traditional societies, such as the Ache, an indigenous people of Paraguay (see Hill & Hurtado, 1996), the level of paternal investment may be positively related to child mortality rates (see Geary, 2005). In developing societies, paternal investment may also have an influence on children's health (see Geary, 2005). For example, a lack of paternal investment has been shown to impact the release of stress hormones in men growing up without fathers (see Flinn et al., 1996). Paternal investment in modern societies may have effects on social and psychological well-being and academic success of children (see Geary, 2005). Paternal investment is also associated with greater upward social mobility of children (Kaplan et al., 1998), perhaps because paternal investment is often indicative of more resource stability and long-term involvement (Flinn et al., 2007). However, paternal care presents potential trade-offs in the father's fitness. These trade-offs require a cost–benefit analysis of the offspring's success or mortality, other mating opportunities, one's own reproductive fitness, and the risk of cuckoldry or paternal uncertainty. Fathers may vary in their level of parental investment due to differences in hormones, genes, quality of their marital relationship, social status, social norms related to polygyny, and the ratio of women to men seeking romantic relationships in their environment (see Geary, 2005).

Extended family members, specifically grandmothers, also contribute to the rearing of young. The saying "it takes a village," when referring to raising a child, is not far from the truth. In pre-westernized societies, child-rearing often falls on all of the women of the village, not just the mother. Sarah Blaffer Hrdy (2009) coined this concept as the *mothers and others* approach, and it is known as the natural approach to child-rearing in humans. Hrdy's approach suggests that in most primate species, including humans in nonindustrialized groups, mothers and other adult female relatives with evolutionarily relevant interests in the offspring are primarily engaged in childcare. Under such conditions, male extended family members typically have a small role in child-rearing. This extended communal care is referred to as *alloparenting* and provides indirect fitness benefits to nonparent relatives (see Geher, 2014; Ko et al., 2020). Specifically, "The Grandmother Hypothesis" suggests that female humans are unique because, although they lose their fertility in later stages of life via menopause, they will still contribute to the rearing of their grandchildren because they know they share a part of their genes (see Hawkes et al., 1998; Ko et al., 2020; Mace, 2015). In both pre-industrialized and modern societies, grandparents, especially maternal grandmothers given their evolutionarily relevant interests, help to enrich the child's social environment by bestowing them with their knowledge and experiences and setting them to be more successful in their social environments (Flinn et al., 2007).

4.2 Mismatch of Modern-Day Child-Rearing

Child-rearing and family lifestyle pertain to another critical aspect of ancestral social conditions that differ from modern day. They also pertain to another area of living where growth and thriving are essential, thus providing a natural nexus of evolutionary and positive psychology. Looking toward Dunbar's theory, it is known that our ancestors all lived within tightly knit communities and were surrounded primarily by kin (Dunbar, 1992). This familial approach differs from how children are raised today in typical westernized nuclear families. In modern society, not only is it common for kin to spread apart from each other geographically, but alloparenting is less of the norm. Most nuclear-family models include dual-income households, with the two parents as the primary providers. Children also tend to be cared for by nonkin strangers at daycare facilities. The isolation from kin members that results from this evolutionary mismatch may cause emotional, physical, and mental stress on both the child and parents. Family is one of the most important aspects of our lives; some evidence even demonstrates that it is rated higher than other life motivations, such as finding romantic partners (Flinn et al., 2007). The lifestyles of ancestral humans may provide valuable information on how we should attempt to organize our familial lives today. Learning from our ancestors, we may be able to enrich our lives, as well as our children's, by staying connected to our relatives and maintaining our strongest familial bonds.

4.3 Applying Evolutionary Principles to Modern Parenting

From ancestral to modern times, family continues to be a central piece and motivator (Flinn et al., 2007) within our lives. Evolutionary principles can be applied to familial bonds to enhance our well-being and livelihood. Specifically, some of these principles can be applied to the ways in which we raise our children (see Geher, 2011). One way to apply evolutionary lessons to parenting is by preparing children to behave altruistically with an awareness of general morality, as if we still lived in our small-scale communities. For instance, teaching children about fairness may be advantageous because our psychology is keenly evolved for the detection of cheaters and social transgressions (Cosmides & Tooby, 1992). Another example relates to reparative altruism. Teaching our children how to repair their relationships and to understand evolutionary relevant emotions like moral outrage may help them to better navigate their relationships when they're older. Overall, these altruistic behaviors can help children to establish the skills to create strong and positive social connections that will be vital for success during their adulthood.

5 Evolutionary Psychology Applied to Education

Through the work of trailblazers such as Geary (Geary & Berch, 2016) and Bjorklund (2023) and others, it has become clear in recent years that the evolutionary perspective has profound implications for understanding child development and the nature of education.

When we look at ancestral childhood development, we see many approaches to raising children, including the *mothers and others* approach (Hrdy, 2009). In such an ancestral approach, villages included both boys and girls interacting with one another, often cutting across various ages. Learning in the nomadic period came primarily from observation and play. This way of learning differs greatly from how children are learning today. Through studying traditional education today, we are beginning to see the "side effects" of this evolutionary mismatch.

The argument of nature versus nurture is often made when discussing the development of children. Some argue that newborns are already primed with all the biological information necessary to predetermine what kind of person they will develop into. Others argue that babies are born as blank slates: that the individuals they surround the child with influence how they will develop. To Bjorklund (2022), it is not so black-and-white. Instead, he argues that infants contain a low level of predetermined cognitive biases that make learning and perceiving certain forms of information more accessible. These information biases can connect with such phenomena as tool-making to relationships and are traits developed during childhood through play and observation (Bjorklund, 2021; Geary, 2005).

We can see examples of this when teaching children how to use utensils. In such a process, children mimic the behavior of their parents, sometimes with encouragement and some informal teaching, and other times through observation (Bjorklund, 2022). While using a fork at the dinner table does not seem like an adaptation, it shows the relevance of using tools. The fear of snakes is a great example of Bjorklund's theory. Those who argue for *nature* argue that this fear is innate. However, a study found that young children are not innately scared of snakes; they do, however, easily acquire an aversion to snakes when they view the fearful expressions of others around snakes (LoBue & Adolph, 2019), seemingly being "prepared" to acquire a fear of snakes. These developmental adaptations have been used for millennia to survive. However, they are not "innate" as some like to think, and they are also not entirely "taught"; they fall somewhere in between. This gray area of learning versus innateness is why education has become so crucial for the development of children. It is also essential to consider the high neuroplasticity levels of children. This cognitive plasticity allows them to adapt better and develop flexibility regarding their environment and events (Bjorklund, 2022).

If you have ever been around a child, you might have noticed how active, playful, curious, and generally sociable they are with the world around them. This is because children show remarkable socio-learning skills enabling them to interact successfully within their cultural norms. These adaptations are rooted in the evolutionary need for socialization (Bjorklund, 2022). Skills such as treating others as *intentional agents* (being able to understand that everything people do has a reason behind it), *shared attention* (two people jointly attending to a third person or object), *emulation* (achieving the same goal as a model but using different behaviors to do so), and *imitation* (copying the behaviors of a model to achieve the same goal as the model) are all considered adaptive traits and are accomplished through informal learning (Tomasello, 2019). However, instructional learning is how most children (school-age especially) are learning today. Instructional learning differs from this more naturally developed learning as it entails the modification of behavior (Bjorklund, 2022). Seeing that such in vivo, hands-on learning tends to be so successful and natural in childhood development, it is both interesting and potentially problematic that early education in schools tends to focus primarily on instructional learning.

This idea of instructional learning tends to contrast the need for play and exploration. There are specific mechanisms that enhance a child's developmental processes. Play and exploration are two of them. While play does decrease with age, in children, it fosters learning and curiosity (Bjorklund, 2022). As *Homo sapiens* have an extended childhood compared to other species of primates, this extension of exploration and play is highly adaptive, as it provides an extended period of time where curiosity and task completion are thoroughly developed and explored (Bjorklund, 2022). In industrialized societies, play is overlooked even though it is so crucial to the successful development of children. For example, in traditional cultures, and surely for our nomadic ancestors, play fighting teaches children social and fighting skills (Bjorklund, 2022). With modern education so focused on instructional learning, it is often suggested that the utilization of more behavior-based, evolutionarily appropriate learning strategies is the better means of education for young children and that allowing children different forms of education, like those seen in nonindustrialized societies, is maladaptive. However, it is found that allowing children to engage in play, specifically fantasy play and exploration, helps with many executive functions such as attention, planning, working memory, language development, and self-regulation (Bjorklund, 2022).

Considering how all these factors speak to developmental learning mechanisms, it is essential to understand how these adaptations might mismatch with the westernized or "WEIRD" (*western, educated, industrial, rich*, and *democratic*) cultural norms or education. The skills developed in nomadic times were primarily learned through observation, as there were very few formal teachings (Bjorklund, 2022). As we have seen in Gray's (2011) work, Bjorklund (2022) reiterates that the mismatches between education development during the nomadic period and today have affected how students learn. In a recent study, Gray (2020) found that during the COVID-19 pandemic, when students were surveyed regarding if they were looking forward to returning to school, around 70 percent said they were. However, it was not the learning aspect of school that they missed but, rather the socialization that they so deeply yearned for. This aligns with what we know regarding childhood development during the nomadic period, where socialization was at the forefront of "education." This comes as no surprise, as scholars have criticized the education system in modern western society for decades. Peter Gray of Boston College documented how mismatched our current education systems are from ancestral conditions (Gray, 2011). Gray found that the United States differs drastically from these pre-industrialized societies when defining education. In pre-industrial cultures, he found that children spend the majority of their days playing outdoors, being supervised by older children, and learning the trades of their communities in that fashion, unlike in typical American classrooms where students sit at desks for eight hours, five days a week, being lectured on basic skills.

We see the negative implications of these teaching methods, specifically with the high diagnosis of boys with attentional issues. On average, boys are diagnosed with attentional problems at rates ten times higher than girls in educational settings (see Geher & Wedberg, 2020). This finding may correspond to

Gray's (2011) finding that in pre-western cultures, boys are found outside running around. Gruskin and Geher (2018) found that college students who had experienced a more evolutionarily typical kind of education style in kindergarten through second grade (free play, natural development of skills and interests) enjoyed school more and did better academically than their peers. When we look at the K-12 educational systems within the United States, for instance, we tend to see a very factory-based approach to education. This approach, as Bjorklund (2022) so eloquently reminds us, is, in so many ways, deeply mismatched from how humans evolved to learn. From a positive evolutionary psychology perspective, we should use what we know about evolutionary development in schools. Bjorklund (2022) recommends allowing students to study things that they enjoy, as well as to foster more evolutionarily relevant activities within modern school systems.

5.1 Technological Mismatch and Supernormal Stimuli Phenomena

Another area where a positive evolutionary psychological approach could be highly useful pertains to technology. In many ways, modern technological advances present arguably the most abrupt evolutionary mismatch between our ancestors and humans today. For instance, by the time a person from a western culture is an adult, it is estimated that they have seen over a thousand instances of violence on TV (see Geher & Wedberg, 2020). These instances can include anything from movies and video games to the atrocities of war, school shootings, and police brutality. Violence is intriguing to people, and viewing violence predisposes people to violent acts (Bildhauer, 2013). In ancestral times, if you were to witness violence or bloodshed, you were in immediate danger and your body reacted accordingly.

Supernormal stimuli (Tinbergen, 1953) pertain to exaggerated forms of stimuli that animals evolved to respond to in certain ways. In modern-day society the idea of supernormal stimuli pertains to how things like horror movies are meant to be exaggerated versions of threatening stimuli, which are meant to engage us in greater behavioral and emotional effects.

When it comes to technology and the idea of evolutionary mismatch, cell phones and social media also contribute to havoc in social contexts. Cell phones are evolutionarily appealing to us because they grant us instant gratification, social connections, unchecked knowledge, and even feed into the drive for sexual reproduction through dating apps. Perhaps interventions designed to decrease screen time (e.g., Khazaei et al., 2017) will ultimately prove beneficial in light of the mismatch that cell phones and other devices (such as cyberbullying) seem to facilitate (see Geher & Wedberg, 2020). Note that social and psychological problems associated with modern technologies are described in detail in a subsequent section 3.

5.2 Mismatch and Positive Evolutionary Psychology Revisited

Importantly, the mismatches found in Sections 5.1 and 3 represent only a slice of the full suite of mismatches that we experience in our daily lives. While this list is preliminary, it can easily be expanded. When we focus on these mismatches and determine the effects that they have on our mental, emotional, developmental, and physical health, researchers and practitioners can think of evolution-based ways to correct the conditions and create positive interventions for society.

6 Evolutionary Psychology, Happiness, and Mental Health

As mentioned in previous sections, positive evolutionary psychology is derived from the fields of evolutionary and positive psychology. Positive evolutionary psychology seeks to improve positive aspects of the human experience, such as positive emotional experiences, positive relationships, positive institutions, and character strengths that allow humans to flourish. These experiences and phenomena include happiness and mental health. As outlined in the US Constitution, one of three foundational rights in any free society is happiness. Happiness is something that people work their entire lives to achieve. Why? Arguably, this is because it is essential to thriving as a human being.

With that in mind, it is obvious that one of the goals of positive psychology would be to cultivate happiness. Factors associated with human happiness have been a large focus of positive psychologists in recent years (see Watkins, 2014). When looking through an evolutionary lens, this makes perfect sense. Charles Darwin himself made the case that humans have evolved to gravitate toward stimuli that facilitate happiness while straying away from stimuli that facilitate things such as anger or sadness (see Darwin, 1872). It is shown through an evolutionary lens that happiness is not bad by any means, but, importantly, that it is a proximate goal rather than an ultimate evolutionary goal. In other words, happiness evolved both for an immediate (proximate) purpose (to make us feel good) as well as for an ultimate purpose (to facilitate our survival and reproduction). Importantly, there are multiple evolutionary-based barriers to achieving happiness, and understanding and acknowledging them is important to be able to work through them to actually achieve happiness. In fact, going all the way back to Darwin (1872), it has been clear that an evolutionary perspective on human emotions suggests that the entire panoply of emotions have their own adaptive functions.

6.1 Anxiety from an Evolutionary Perspective

Despite humans being evolved largely to seek happiness, it is important to recognize that things such as anxiety and fear have their place too. Randolph Nesse gave a presentation at the State University of New York at New Paltz in 2017 that included an anecdote that lays out the nature of happiness extremely well. The story was essentially as follows:

> A while ago, Nesse had a client who was a professor. This professor was dealing with issues of anxiety, like so many of us do. Nesse prescribed the client antianxiety medication. A few months later, Nesse checked in with the professor on how he was feeling, and the professor said that for the first time in years he felt great. Despite feeling great, he mentioned he had one problem: he had a huge stack of student papers that had been needing grading for weeks, but he had no motivation to grade them.

In his work on evolutionary medicine (Nesse & Williams, 1995), Nesse made the case that symptoms, whether physical or emotional, tend to exist for evolutionary reasons, and that any medical approaches to stop the symptoms are potentially naïve and possibly problematic. In this case, it seems that the anxiety the professor was experiencing played a motivational factor in his life, despite their unpleasantness.

In fact, from an evolutionary perspective, motivation is pretty much the ultimate reason anxiety exists at all (Nesse & Ellsworth, 2009). Anxiety plays a role in motivating people to take adaptive actions. In ancestral times, people likely became anxious in situations where their lives were in danger, their social life was threatened, and so on. Ancestors who showed no anxiety to these types of scenarios would never have taken the appropriate steps to fix the problem or threat.

Anxiety is not pleasant, but it does serve a purpose. It is important to remember that because eliminating it entirely, as demonstrated by the anecdote given by Nesse, can actually be maladaptive.

6.2 Happiness as a Proximate Goal

As mentioned in Section 6.1, happiness is not an ultimate evolutionary goal but rather a proximate goal. From an evolutionary perspective, human emotions have evolved because they generally have evolutionary benefits: increasing the probability of survival or reproductive capacities (see Guitar et al., 2018). Happiness has evolved to increase adaptive behaviors the same way anxiety has evolved to increase adaptive behaviors.

If you think about things that make people happy, you can clearly see that they generally match up to outcomes that would lead to increased probability of survival and reproduction for our ancestors: things such as food, sex, fun times with friends, social success, task completion (Geher & Wedberg, 2020). Looking at that small list, it is clear that these kinds of outcomes have the capacity to lead to happiness as well as clear adaptive evolutionary benefits.

So the evolutionary take on happiness is basically as follows: happiness is an affective state that motivates us to engage in actions that are likely to lead to outcomes that would, on average, lead to increases in the likelihood of survival or reproduction (Guitar et al., 2018). In evolutionary terms, we would say, then, that happiness is a proximate outcome. It is important, but it is not an ultimate evolutionary goal.

From an evolutionary perspective, happiness is not the end goal; it is a *means to an end* (Geher & Wedberg, 2020). Despite happiness and positive psychology being a more recent focus in the field, happiness is something we have been achieving and experiencing since ancestral times. The recent focus on happiness in today's society has come about due to the modern barriers to improving quality of life and experiencing happiness as outlined by Buss (2000). Buss named three barriers to happiness: (a) discrepancies between modern and ancestral environments; (b) evolved mechanisms that lead to subjective distress; and (c) competitive mechanisms that have been produced by selection. These three barriers make achieving happiness incredibly difficult, but Buss gives multiple evolutionary-based strategies to help break down and ameliorate each of these.

The first of these barriers is one that is considered to be a foundational concept in evolutionary psychology as discussed see Section 3 in this Element, evolutionary mismatch. Despite the benefits and comforts of modern environments, discrepancies from ancient contexts can create situations that make happiness and mental well-being much more difficult to achieve than in ancestral times. There is evidence that rates of depression are actually increasing in modern and more developed life (e.g., Twenge, 2017). The question is, why?

There are multiple hypotheses that might be able to explain this. For example, Nesse and Williams (1995) proposed that the relative anonymity and isolated nuclear families are depriving people of intimate social support that characterized social conditions in ancestral times. People in modern societies spread out in pursuit of work, opportunities, love, and so on, leaving families scattered across countries and continents. Another hypothesis proposed by Nesse and Williams (1995) is that there is an increase in perceived self-failures that result from erroneous comparisons between people's own lives and the lives they see people living in the media. We no longer compare ourselves to our small group of 50 to 150 people (Dunbar, 1992); we now compare ourselves to millions of people throughout the world on social media, television, and the Internet.

Seeing all of these different people and their lives causes us to be envious and set goals for ourselves in order to achieve the fantasies we see. The problem is the goals we set in an attempt to live life like television characters or Internet influencers are not realistic or achievable in everyday life. Therefore, we are left feeling inadequate and as if we have failed. These are just a few of many examples that support the concept of discrepancies in modern and ancestral environments as a barrier to happiness.

The second barrier mentioned by Buss is evolved mechanisms that lead to subjective distress. These mechanisms are designed to solve a specific adaptive problem, but in other situations cause subjective stress; jealousy is a good example of this. There is much empirical evidence for the idea of jealousy as an evolved psychological mechanism to alert someone of a partner's infidelity, whether actual or perceived (Daly & Wilson, 1997; Symons 1979). Subjectively, jealousy can be an extremely distressing emotion. In common culture it is referred to as the *green-eyed monster* because once it is felt it does not stop until the issue is resolved. It can cause sleepless nights, cause someone to question their worth, create anxiety about losing their partner, and completely shake up social reputation. Despite all of the negative feelings that go along with jealousy, it motivated beneficial adaptive change in our ancestors and served enough of a purpose that its pitfalls have been overlooked. This same concept is applied to other mechanisms that cause subjective stress.

The third and last barrier that Buss attributed to the impediment of happiness is adaptions that are designed for competition. This barrier stems from the Buss's concept of competition, or differential reproductive success, because competition is seen as the "engine of the evolutionary process" (Buss, 2000, p. 18). In mechanisms evolved for competition, one person's gain is typically another person's loss. Think about gossip, which seems to have a function of making a potential intrasexual rival less desirable in order to boost one's own personal status in the relationship market.

Although it is important to understand the possible reasons for the impediment of happiness, it is even more important to know how to overcome these barriers and what steps we can take toward achieving happiness. Buss (2000) provided many provocative ideas for achieving happiness, including the following:

- Closing the gap between modern and ancestral times
- Increasing closeness of extended kin
- Developing deep friendships
- Selecting a mate who is similar to oneself
- Managing competitive mechanisms
- The fulfillment of basic biological desires

6.3 Motivation and Human Needs

The study of human motivation and needs goes back decades, with perhaps the most famous exemplar found in the groundbreaking work of Abraham Maslow (1943). Understanding human needs is, in fact, critical for understanding the entirety of the human experience.

Importantly, while the emerging area of positive evolutionary psychology represents an explicit and cutting-edge effort to address issues of the human condition with an eye toward positive growth, our work in this area does not represent the first or only effort on this front. In *Solving Modern Problems with a Stone Age Brain*, Kenrick and Lundberg-Kenrick (2022) prolifically draw on evolutionary principles to shed light on issues of human growth, integrating evolutionary themes (such as the importance of reproductive success in shaping so much of human behavior) with Maslow's (1943) famous model of human needs. In doing so, Kenrick and Lundberg-Kenrick (2022) cite behavioral spheres, such as successful mating and parenting, as including critical evolved needs that bear on human growth, happiness, and self-actualization. Similarly, Kaufman (2020) drew on a broad array of psychological concepts, including various basic evolutionary principles, in developing a similarly Maslowian model of human potential, growth, and (per his book's title) *Transcend*.

While Maslow himself did not actually depict his model with a graphical pyramid (see Kaufman, 2020), the pyramid metaphor, adopted by Kenrick and Lundberg-Kenrick (2022), is useful for understanding the idea that some needs are more basic than are others. For Maslow, starting with the most foundational needs, the primary human needs are as follows:

- Physiological needs
- Safety needs
- Belongingness needs
- Love needs
- Esteem needs
- Self-actualization

While this model certainly includes variables that bear on evolutionary themes (e.g., safety needs), unlike the model advanced by Kenrick and Lundberg-Kenrick (2022), the model was not premised inherently on evolutionary principles.

The model advanced most recently by Kenrick and Lundberg-Kenrick (2022) is, importantly, an evolutionarily informed model – and one that bears closely on the goals of positive evolutionary psychology. In order of how basic each need is in this model, the primary needs are as follows:

- Physiological needs
- Self-protection
- Affiliation
- Status/Esteem
- Mate Acquisition
- Mate Retention
- Parenting

A primary difference between these models pertains to the emphasis that Kenrick and Lundberg-Kenrick place on reproductive success as something of an ultimate goal. This focus is largely found in the importance of mating and parenting, which are, from an evolutionary perspective, essentially sine qua non when it comes to advancing one's genes into the future. While Maslow focused largely on an individual's own subjective well-being, using an approach that draws importantly on the evolutionary psychology literature, Kenrick and Lundberg-Kenrick's (2022) model focuses, rather, on needs that would have advanced survival and reproductive goals under ancestral conditions. From this perspective, phenomena such as self-actualization are actually quite secondary relative to needs that ultimately, on average, led to reproductive success under ancestral human conditions. And it is this latter approach that so strongly maps onto the basic ideas of positive evolutionary psychology that are addressed in this Element.

6.4 Mental Health and Modern Technology

As mentioned in a previous section, evolutionary mismatch is often at the core of psychological problems. People become addicted and reliant on human-made technologies, which have been found to be associated with a whole list of negative psychological and physical outcomes (Twenge, 2017). In her years of work on this topic, Twenge (2017) labels these individuals as comprising the Internet Generation, comprised of people who were born between about 1995 and 2005. This is the first generation in the entire human experience for whom the Internet and related technologies have always existed. Such a life inherently is filled with mismatches, as such technologies are deeply mismatched from ancestral communication systems that surrounded our evolutionary history (see Geher & Wedberg, 2020). From this perspective, it is little wonder that the Internet Generation has seen relatively high levels of mental health issues.

With any technological advance, the purpose is to improve the human experience, and the Internet has done so in many ways. On the other hand, technology may also be contributing to the current mental health crisis. This contribution to the mental health crisis may be due to the deindividuated communication that is often occurring–think about how deindividuated people are on the Internet. Individuals of this Internet Generation are constantly interacting with people from all over the world remotely, so even if they are interacting with someone they know, they are still behind a screen. A standard finding in social psychological literature is that people act in a relatively antisocial manner when their identities are anonymous (see Figueredo et al., 2006; Zimbardo, 2007). Basically, what all of this means is that it is much easier for people to be mean to one another than it ever has been before, thanks to the Internet. Mean and hurtful outcomes can, without question, have detrimental negative effects on mental health.

With the easy access to Internet technologies, this Internet Generation is experiencing a multitude of adverse consequences that are likely to have long-term effects on a global scale. Understanding our psychology from an evolutionary perspective is essential to understanding the foundational reasons for this concerning trend.

7 Evolutionary Psychology and the Cultivation of Community

Unlike other hominins, ancestral *Homo sapiens* evolved to establish relationships beyond kin-lines, which have allowed them to form large-scale groups (Bingham & Souza, 2009). These community-building skills may have been a key factor in our evolutionary large-scale proliferation as a species because they allow for large-scale cooperation and teamwork in accomplishing goals that cannot be achieved independently. Without community, humankind would not have been able to collaborate to cultivate the technologies, large cities, and globalization that exist today. It is our fundamental tendency to create larger, social worlds, beyond our familial ties, that make us human.

7.1 Our Social Nature

Humans are an extraordinarily social and group-oriented species. Adaptations such as linguistic skills, mental representation, theory of mind, self-awareness, and social learning (Flinn et al., 2007) have allowed for the development of complex social groups. Although the human body is slow to develop, our brains develop rapidly and are flexible to changes in our environment. Linguistic capabilities, which develop rapidly and early in our lives, are especially vital in navigating complex social interactions and cultural norms (Dunbar, 1998; Pinker, 1994). One of the most salient selective pressures for humans is social competition. Brain structures and cognitive processes designed to help us form alliances, keep track of social contracts, and partake in reciprocal altruism would have been adaptive to combat the evolutionary pressures within the intricate social world we have created.

7.2 Reciprocal Altruism

Our ability to establish relationships that extend beyond familial ties is rooted in our prosocial behavior, particularly in reciprocal altruism (Trivers, 1971). Unlike kin-selected altruism, which is helping behavior found between genetically related individuals, reciprocal altruism occurs between unrelated individuals as a mechanism to return favors. While cooperation among kin increases indirect fitness benefits by increasing the genetic fitness of an individual's relatives (Hamilton, 1964), reciprocal altruism can provide direct and immediate fitness benefits to the individual. For instance, research studying food exchange in a forager-horticulturalist population on an Ache reservation showed that Ache households prefer sharing food with kin who have helped the household in the past over kin who do not reciprocate helping behavior. Although the Ache prefer helping their kin over nonkin, they prioritize reciprocating with helpful kin because they play a larger role in providing direct fitness (Allen-Arave et al., 2008). Cultivating a reputation of generosity was also observed as a method to increase an individual's social and practical advantages, such as with food sharing. This research demonstrates that reciprocal altruism is paramount in developing a strong social network that can help to increase individual fitness (Allen-Arave et al., 2008).

Our altruistic ancestors profited from these reciprocal exchanges by essentially expecting payback from other reliable, cooperative individuals. The implicit understanding that an individual will be helped in the future by another conspecific encourages people to engage in altruistic behavior toward others (Trivers, 1971). Some characteristics of relationships, such as proximity, familiarity, and trust, increase the probability of reciprocal altruism (Allen-Arave et al., 2008). Knowing a conspecific well enough to trust them and expect that they will cooperate in the future increases the inclination of helping behavior. Helping individuals whom one is likely to encounter multiple times in the future also increases the probability of receiving aid. Through reciprocal altruism and our implicit social contracts, we facilitate our own survival by helping our conspecifics. Reciprocal altruism helps to form alliances and other kinds of relationships which can later develop into communities. The evolutionary psychology of reciprocal altruism helps us to understand thriving at the community level, thus explicating a true exemplar of positive evolutionary psychology.

7.3 Defining Features of Evolved Human Communities

Community has promoted our survival since ancestral times and has, thus, become fundamental to human psychology and behavior. There are a few key defining features that have helped communities to thrive throughout our evolutionary history. For instance, communities often share goals that they can work toward together. Our ancestors may have formed communities to hunt and gather food, raise children, and build shelters. According to David Sloan Wilson's (2007) research on multilevel selection, certain cooperative behaviors may have been selected to help build communities beyond kin-lines, and our groups often operate as a single unit or organism. Our ability to form alliances and work collectively with nonkin members contributes not only to the evolutionary success and social functioning of a group as a whole but also to the thriving and evolutionary success of the individual. In other words, what benefits the group often also benefits the individual by increasing their chances of survival and reproductive success (Wilson, 2007). Overall, ancestors who were a part of a decently sized, collaborative group were likely to outcompete other groups for resources with fewer members and less intergroup cooperation.

Another feature that has facilitated our survival and has allowed communities to develop is norms related to reciprocal altruism and other social exchanges. Norms related to reciprocal altruism entail that in order to receive support in the future, one must uphold their end of a social contract by behaving altruistically toward those who have helped them in the past. Human communities evolved under small-scale conditions and, as is noted in a prior Section 3.1, they usually reached capacity at Dunbar's number of 150 individuals (Dunbar, 1992). These ecological conditions allowed for small-scale communities to easily keep track of these norms and social exchanges. Our ancestors often diligently kept track of their social contracts, which allowed them to adapt multiple cognitive skills and social behaviors for cheater-detection (Cosmides & Tooby, 1992). Ancestors who cultivated a helper-reputation were likely to receive the benefits of their community, while ancestors who broke their social contacts and cheated others were likely to be punished by their community.

Because much of our survival is dependent on social support from other group members, communities evolved to maintain strong interpersonal cooperation. Some of our skills for cooperation, especially within our tightly knit groups, resulted from our ability to learn how to resolve conflict and reconcile with others. According to a review on violence and conflict resolution by de Waal (2002), many species of primate, as well as humans, tend to demonstrate collective intercommunity violence. However, the way we resolve conflict within our close communities often overcomes the evolutionary challenges of aggression and the potential loss of integral social networks.

Humans often engage in reconciliatory social behaviors to avoid continuous conflict and severing crucial social ties. In fact, humans, as well as multiple species of primates, will attempt to counteract the social harm caused by aggression by actively seeking contact with the individuals they, or their kin, had wronged. On some occasions, as noted in chimpanzees, a third-party member will try to make amends by bringing two offenders together (see Trivers, R. (1985). Social Evolution. Benjamin/Cummings.) Similar patterns have been found in humans. For instance, cross-culturally, many communities and societies, including semi-sedentary ethnic groups like the Mayalan Semai, demonstrate a preference for harmony and cooperation over interpersonal conflict (de Waal, 2002). The probability that an individual is likely to reconcile with another individual is largely dependent on the strength and security of the relationship, implying that the value of mutual aid has been evaluated as more significant than the damage inflicted by the parties involved in the aggression. Overall, our evolved mechanisms and inclinations to repair our close relationships ensure that our most valued relationships and inner communities will be prioritized. This conception of forgiveness as having deep evolutionary roots has been documented extensively by Michael McCullough and others (e.g., McCauley et al., 2022), suggesting that forgiveness and related social-emotional processes are, in fact, deeply rooted in our evolutionary heritage.

Because of our keen record keeping of social exchanges, communities are evolutionarily different from other types of groups in that they often operate as a network of support systems. Communities foster the fulfillment of social contacts and reciprocation of helping behavior. The support one of our ancestors would have received from their conspecifics in a tightly knit, functional community would have largely contributed to their thriving and well-being. To this day, developing community – a support system of individuals who consistently reciprocate and keep a record of favors – allows an individual to reach goals that will sustain a positive, connected, and social lifestyle.

7.4 Modern Communities: Neighborhoods as Communities

Although modern populations vastly exceed the scope of the ancestral world, reciprocal altruism and strong social contracts continue to be markers of strongly unified and harmonious communities. Additionally, community building in our modern environment persists to be a way for us to achieve large goals and tasks, to network with others, and to create extended families. Modern communities often share a similar identity, unifying purpose, or a nearby geographical location. Examples of modern communities include, and are not limited to, religious groups, academic committees, research labs, political groups, and neighborhoods.

Neighborhoods have often been the focus of research in understanding the psychological and social benefits of community when utilizing an evolutionary perspective. For example, David Sloan Wilson and Dan O'Brien's (2011) research on neighborhoods located in Binghamton, New York, has shed light on how communal behavior varies across different communities and is influenced by the strength of our relationships and interconnectedness (see O'Brien & Wilson, 2011; Wilson, 2011). Their research mainly highlights the relationship between neighbor-related behavior and social capital. Social capital refers to the value or strength of social relationships and is defined in several ways. Wilson and O'Brien operationalized social capital in their research by examining how neighborhoods decorate their homes during the holidays, specifically during Christmas.

According to their findings, individuals living in neighborhoods, who feel safe and interconnected to their neighbors, tend to display more social capital in the form of maintaining the appearance of the exterior of their homes. Mainly, Wilson and O'Brien found that these neighbors tend to put up more festive decorations outside of their homes during the holiday season. Contrarily, individuals who live in neighborhoods with low ratings of feelings of security and connectedness to their neighbors tend to showcase less of these kinds of social capital. People in such reclusive neighborhoods also tend to put less effort into the aesthetics of their neighborhood, such as the upkeep of their yards, sidewalks, and streetlights. Fascinatingly, these differences were found in a range of neighborhoods, despite their socioeconomic status, meaning that the wealth of these communities had little effect on the neighbors' display of social capital. In other words, two communities with equal socioeconomic status could look visually very different depending not just on their wealth, but on the strength of their sense of community. These findings suggest that social capital is an important way for modern humans to distinguish their community's identity from other communities and to maintain a level of security.

In another study conducted under the auspices of the Boston Area Research Initiative, O'Brien, Giordon, and Phillipi-Baldwin (2014) analyzed people's willingness to engage in custodial behavior within their neighborhoods. Custodial behavior refers to the active engagement in prosocial behaviors that will benefit and maintain the security of a community. This study operational-ized custodial behavior as the number of calls to the city's 311 hotline in a given neighborhood. The city's hotline is used to report problems in the city that warrant attention, but are not emergencies, such as vandalized property and noise complaints. O'Brien and his research team used GPS technology to track the patterns of 311 calls.

O'Brien and colleagues found that few people – roughly 3–6 percent – engaged in custodial behavior in their neighborhood. However, these patterns of custodial behavior tended to be specific to the caller's neighborhood. That is, people were more likely to use the 311 hotline to report issues in their own neighborhood than in another neighborhood. These findings demonstrate that prosocial behavior has geographical limits. From an evolutionary perspective, this finding is sensible, as it would have been more beneficial for one of our ancestors to help a nearby conspecific who could reciprocate in the future rather than another individual whom they would likely never meet again. Overall, these studies help to understand how community benefits the individual in terms of safety, identity, and social connection.

7.5 Implications for Positive Psychology

Positive communities, from an evolutionary paradigm, are marked by altruism, kindness, collaboration, and cooperation. Individuals who are members of communities that contain these features are able to develop a sense of security and safety, feelings of interconnectedness, and strong support systems that extend beyond familial relationships. Acts of kindness and altruism not only help to cultivate positive communities but they also function to improve individual, emotional well-being. For instance, much research has found that giving to others feels emotionally good, both on the receiving and giving end (e.g., Underwood et al., 1977). If community building is ingrained in human psychology and improves our emotional well-being, it is important for us to stay connected in order to live a fulfilled life. Humans can stay proactive in their communities via collaboration, altruism, custodial behavior, and acts of kindness, in order to live out more positive lives and to receive the socioemotional benefits of community.

8 The Evolution of Social and Moral Emotions

Because of our deep history of reciprocal altruism (see DeJesus et al., 2021), we evolved a broad suite of moral emotions that serve the function of helping people stay connected to others within communities. From this perspective, guilt evolved to motivate reparative behaviors after someone has trespassed on someone else's person or family. Forgiveness evolved as a way to accept someone, in spite of past trespasses or imperfections, back into the fold of the broader community.

Another critical feature of our evolved moral psychology is found in pride, which may be seen as a social and moral emotion that allows us to monitor other peoples' perceptions of our own social value. As discussed in prior sections, much of our survival in the environment of evolutionary adaptiveness was dependent on the quality of our relationships and assistance from our group members. Obtaining respect and being valued by other people likely enhanced our social networks, thus improving our chances of survival and reproductive success. Positive evaluations act as an evolutionary resource by increasing access to available social support and increasing the frequency of prosocial interactions. The ability to regulate one's behavior in response to other individuals' explicit or implicit assessments of oneself would have been adaptive.

Thus, pride may be thought of as a critical social emotion that runs deep in human history. From an evolutionary perspective, pride may have evolved to modulate behaviors that are likely to increase other individuals' respect and valuation of ourselves (Sznycer et al., 2017; Sznycer et al., 2018). According to this conceptualization of pride, also known as the *advertisement–recalibration theory of pride*, pride recruits various cognitive processes and provokes certain physiological responses when assessing the potential value or cost of a behavior. The feeling of pride is highly pleasurable (Mauro et al., 1992), motivating us to engage in socially rewarding behaviors and to advertise our favorable characteristics and actions (Williams & DeSteno, 2008). An appropriate display of pride may also help to attract mates, because pride behaviors signal certain fitness indicators, such as social capital (Sznycer et al., 2017).

Although there may be some cultural differences in what values elicit pride, there are many universal facets of pride. Across cultures, pride tends to emerge during specific developmental periods, manifest in recognizable displays, and is often triggered by achievements and behaviors that enhance one's social value (Sznycer et al., 2017). In two separate studies, one using a sample of sixteen different countries (Sznycer et al., 2017), and another using ten small-scale communities worldwide (Sznycer et al., 2018), Sznycer and colleagues found that pride is distinctly involved in the enhancement and monitoring of social valuation. These cross-cultural findings suggest that pride is universal and has evolutionary functions. However, it is important to note that appropriate expressions of pride are necessary in order to maintain high valuations. For instance, not experiencing enough pride decreases self-advertisement of potentially valued traits. Alternatively, experiencing too much pride over-advertises the self, which is especially unfavorable in instances when pride is unwarranted (Sznycer et al., 2017). Therefore, our cognitive systems for pride must be sensitive to our audiences' evaluations.

Unlike many of the other-oriented emotions studied in positive psychology, such as compassion and gratitude, pride tends to be conceptualized as a self-focused emotion (Haidt, 2003). However, the self-evaluation component of pride is very other-oriented as it requires an understanding and anticipation of others' evaluations of oneself. The self-evaluation aspect of pride not only serves to improve one's hierarchical position, but also ultimately enriches one's social network and relationships. For instance, one study found that in comparison to other moral emotions, pride most strongly predicts moral choices in prosocial situations (Krettenauer et al., 2011). Other lines of research also suggest that pride is associated with motivating other-oriented, prosocial behaviors (Michie, 2009; Nakamura, 2013; Verbeke et al., 2004). More specifically, the experience of pride has been tied to prosocial behaviors and feelings of everyday purpose in family life, particularly in caring for offspring, and in the work setting, when successfully assisting one's clients (Nakamura, 2013).

In general, pride is positively associated with feelings of self-esteem (Tracy et al., 2009) and feelings of achievement and purpose in life (see Carver et al., 2010). From a positive psychological perspective, pride has been documented to indirectly improve well-being through agency motivation (Barrett-Cheetham et al., 2016). Meanwhile, an evolutionary perspective of pride accentuates the ways pride reinforces fitness enhancing and socially valued behaviors such as altruism. As a moral and social emotion, pride has the potential to strengthen our relationships, enhance our perceived social worth and value, increase self-esteem, and create meaning in our lives. However, the positive implications of pride and its intersections with evolutionary psychology require further research and investigation. To properly study pride through a positive evolutionary psychological lens, the emotion needs to be addressed in populations cross-culturally, especially in non-WEIRD and pre-industrialized societies. Distinctions between the positive implications of pride as a self-oriented achievement and as a reinforcer of prosocial behavior are also warranted.

9 Evolutionary Psychology and Physical Health

As described in Section 3, evolutionary mismatch is the idea that our society today is greatly different compared to the everyday society that our ancestors lived in. Thus, we lead very different lives in a very different environment compared to our ancestors. These mismatches can cause both physical and behavioral problems and we see great examples when speaking in terms of our physical health (see Cordain et al., 2005; Wolf, 2010).

9.1 Positive Evolutionary Psychology and Our Physical Health

Under modern, westernized conditions, we see a huge evolutionary mismatch in humans and physical health. One of the most prominent mismatches has to do with exercise. Back in our evolutionary history we were nomadic hunter gatherers, meaning our ancestors moved around a lot. They moved around to ensure their safety, they followed their food, and in doing so would get their exercise via this traveling as well as through hunting and gathering. Biological anthropologists have estimated the average nomadic group would travel nearly twenty miles a day (see Geher & Wedberg, 2020). Now, think about today. The average American, five days a week, sits working a desk job just to go home and sit on the couch to relax for the night. Sure, some people sneak a trip to the gym a couple times a week and walk an average of about one to two miles, but this is not nearly as much exercise as our ancestors were getting. For most contemporary people, even the commute to work involves more sitting, as the majority of us travel via car or bus. To many Americans, exercising is a burden or a chore rather than a means of survival. We are living an increasingly sedentary lifestyle, and that is a huge daily mismatch.

This lifestyle became more sedentary due to the COVID-19 pandemic. When the pandemic hit, schools as well as jobs switched to becoming completely online. So now, the commute to work could be as little as walking from the bed to the couch. As more people work remotely, there is often no reason for many people to get out of the house on a daily basis. Exercise is increasingly important for both physical and mental well-being. Positive psychology is largely focused around mental and physical health, which are largely connected with exercise. Thus, increasing exercise advances the goals of positive psychology in light of the evolutionarily relevant concept of mismatch. In fact, various researchers have documented that an evolutionary approach to exercise has all kinds of health-related benefits (see Bjorklund, 2022; Fell & Geher, 2018; Platek et al., 2011).

In their work on this topic, both Platek et al. (2011) and Fell and Geher (2018) found evidence that the use of exercise regimens that were devised using evolutionary principles (such as CrossFit) tend to include more holistic forms of exercise and tend to lead to better outcomes than those found in more traditional exercise regimens. For instance, a typical CrossFit workout might include dragging a large tire across a field, in an effort to mirror an experience such as dragging recently hunted game back to camp. That kind of activity is clearly quite different than, for example, doing a set of bench presses. CrossFit activities are largely designed to be functional in nature, as physical activity during the human EEA was generally functional (e.g., hunting, moving from one camp to another). Related, CrossFit, compared with many standard exercise regimens, has an inherently social element to it, as an attempt to mirror the fact that under ancestral conditions, people were generally engaging in physical activities in coordination with others.

Fell and Geher (2018) found that, relative to individuals who had the Gold's Gym experience, individuals who adopted the CrossFit experience showed improvements that extended beyond the physical: in many cases, these individuals reported social and emotional improvements as well. In short, adopting ancestrally appropriate forms of exercise seems to have health benefits across the board.

9.2 Positive Evolutionary Psychology and Diet

Another way we see evolutionary mismatch in our physical health is found in our diet and the food we consume. Back under ancestral human conditions, finding food that was sugary and high in fat was a rare treat. Foods high in fat and sugar were highly desired for survival as it was a way to gain body fat to prepare for a drought which oftentimes brought famine. We have this same desire for sugary fatty foods in our current conditions, with popular fast-food chains dominating the food industry. With nearly 200,000 fast-food establishments in the United States, we have a real problem on our hands (Diraddo, 2022). Fast-food chains such as McDonalds, Burger King, and Wendy's are highly recognized and get a plethora of business, earning about $278.6 billion in revenue in 2021 alone (Diraddo, 2022). These establishments continue to get massive business despite it being well-known that the food they serve is not necessarily healthy or good for us. When we look at this from a positive evolutionary psychology standpoint, it makes sense why we are so drawn to these foods. Getting these foods in our evolutionary history meant survival, and survival meant that an individual could reproduce and pass on their genes. We are, in a sense, wired to be attracted to these fatty and sugary foods. But nowadays, with the abundant changes in our lifestyle and environment, ironically, this abundance of processed food is a catalyst for heart conditions, obesity, and resultant diseases like diabetes. These sugary, processed foods being more available and less expensive than natural foods is also a contributing factor to people being pushed into unhealthy eating habits. The best way to try to tackle this mismatch is to have a diet with foods that would align with and be available under our ancestral conditions.

Why should we care about these mismatches? And what does it have to do with positive evolutionary psychology? Thinking about it simply, this is the only body we get. There are no do-overs. Positive psychology focuses heavily on the idea of thriving. If an individual can align their daily life with some aspects from our ancestral history, they will see that they can achieve this goal of thriving and lead a better, more successful life.

9.3 The Common Cold

Another way we see an impact of positive evolutionary psychology on our physical health is when we take a look at the human body and diseases. Think about an individual who is sick with a cold and running a fever. The first thing they will probably do is take Tylenol or Advil to get the fever to go down.

But when we take a step back and think about fevers in an evolutionary scope, they are often beneficial. The body is fighting off foreign invaders, and to do so it increases the body's temperature to kill viruses and heal. Under ancestral conditions there was no Tylenol, no Advil, and no amoxicillin. The body was solely in charge of getting the individual better, and the body is (for the most part) good at its job. So when someone takes things like Tylenol, they are keeping their body from getting them better. As stated in our book on this topic (Geher & Wedberg, 2020), optimal health does not always mean that one *feels good*.

Importantly, note that we are not advocating a case against modern medicine. Indeed, modern medicine has proven to have all kinds of positive benefits when it comes to human health. What we are advocating, rather, is evolution training for health professionals so that insights from evolution can help shed light on how members of the health professions treat illnesses.

9.4 Expectant Mothers

The same principle can apply for pregnant women. One of the most dreaded symptoms that comes with being pregnant is nausea. Oftentimes expectant mothers experiencing pregnancy sickness will go to their doctor and get prescribed medication to help stop pregnancy sickness. But once again step back and take a look through the evolutionary psychology scope. Starting with a little history lesson, most of the medications that were created and administered for pregnancy sickness were later shown to have adverse effects on the growing child (Geher & Wedberg, 2020). So why were we so quick to develop a medication to stop this symptom? What if there was a benefit to the mothers getting sick? Evolutionary biologist Margie Profet (1997) hypothesized that pregnancy sickness is a mechanism to protect the embryo. The mother physically expels foods as a way of protecting the unborn child from foods that could contain chemicals and bacteria that could be harmful and toxic to the growing embryo. Although pregnancy sickness is not a great way to start or end the day, it has an evolutionary purpose. Keeping the developing child away from potentially toxic and harmful chemicals and bacteria helps to ensure their survival, which in turn passes on the individual's genes and leads them yet again to the goal of thriving.

Positive evolutionary psychology has a great deal to do with our everyday physical health, and it is important that we understand this. The more we understand, the more likely we are to thrive and be happy and healthy in our everyday lives. So the next time you want to skip a workout, eat McDonalds for the third night in a row, or reach for that bottle of medication stop and think: What would our ancestors do?

10 Future Directions in Positive Evolutionary Psychology

The future of positive evolutionary psychology is far-reaching. Merging the fields of positive psychology and evolutionary psychology has led to more ways to understand the growth of human behavior and how we can positively impact aspects of the human experience. By using an evolutionary lens to analyze behaviors specific to the modern human, we can see where we are being negatively affected as a result of our digression from the ancestral human way of living. Positive evolutionary psychology can help us turn negative aspects of the human experience into positive ones.

The ever-growing field of evolutionary psychology has had, at times, a controversial reputation in academia (Confer et al., 2010), as mentioned See Section 1 in this Element. Furthermore, some academics critique evolutionary psychology for being too deterministic (Grinde, 2002), while other critiques stem from misunderstandings regarding the rationale behind evolutionary psychology and its misuse. Positive evolutionary psychology can help to eliminate the disconnect between traditional psychological perspectives and the evolutionary perspective. The two share many more similarities than one may initially think. Positive psychologists study the factors that contribute to life satisfaction with the goal of helping people lead richer lives (Gable & Haidt, 2005). The same outlook can be applied to evolutionary psychology. The integration of positive evolutionary psychology in our modern lives, in areas such as happiness, mental health, physical health, and the cultivation of community, can allow us to connect to ourselves and the world around us by using the knowledge of our ancestral ways of living and in turn allow us to lead richer lives.

10.1 Adverse Consequences of Mismatch in the Modern World

One of the most critical concepts within positive evolutionary psychology bears on the topic of evolutionary mismatch – a concept that is featured heavily in this piece. This is for good reason. Much of our dissatisfaction with life can be credited to the mismatch between the modern lifestyle and that of our ancestors. As described previously in this Element, evolutionary mismatches occur when the conditions of the modern environment do not align with those of our ancestors' environment, also known as the environment of evolutionary adaptedness; therefore, traits that were once beneficial to us may now be maladaptive. No one individual is at fault for this mismatch, since we continue to evolve on a societal and global level, which is out of one's control. However, there are things we can do as individuals to decrease life dissatisfaction that is a product of modern, western ways of living. This is by no means an easy task, as we have become accustomed to the luxuries this lifestyle provides for us; but by changing just one aspect of our life, overall happiness can drastically increase. By living in accordance with features of ancestral social and physical conditions, we can eliminate factors that contribute to mental health disturbances (e.g., anxiety), sickness (e.g., type-II diabetes), and the feeling of estrangement from friends and family and increase behaviors that help our overall well-being and heighten happiness.

10.2 Emotional States from a Positive Evolutionary Psychology Perspective

Another bottom-line issue that emerges when thinking about positive evolutionary psychology pertains to the very nature of human emotions. The capacity to experience both positive and negative emotional states is something unique to *Homo sapiens*, as shaped by our evolutionary history (Grinde, 2002). Most other animals have not genetically inherited as sophisticated a capacity for this as humans have. Future research should aim to tease out how happiness is both built into our DNA and constructed by ourselves/our environment. This distinction will allow us to better understand the ways in which positive evolutionary psychology can come into play, as intervention is much more accessible when there are factors we can control as individuals. It is important to note that it is impossible to lay the responsibility for our happiness solely in the hands of evolutionary psychology, as it is unavoidably an indirect consequence of human nature.

As described in prior sections, happiness can be difficult to achieve when we are faced with the hardships of daily life, such as mental illness. According to the National Alliance on Mental Illness (NAMN), one in five (52.9 million) adults experience mental illness in the United States (National Alliance on Mental Illness, 2022). The NAMN found that anxiety disorders are the most common mental illness, affecting 19.1 percent (48 million) of people. We discussed in a previous section of this Element that anxiety is an evolutionary adaptation. Our ancestors constantly had to be on the lookout for predators, so adapting anxiety tendencies helped them survive. Although we no longer need to be anxious about becoming lunch for a saber-tooth tiger, the modern world has many other anxiety-inducing factors, which is why this adaptation has stuck around. Anxiety exists for important reasons. And evolutionary psychology can help us understand why.

10.3 The Altricial Human

Another basic concept from this Element that speaks to the foundational ideas of positive evolutionary psychology pertains to human altriciality. The large-scale proliferation of *Homo sapiens* can be greatly attributed to the human ability to work together. Evolving from small communities where we lived in groups ranging from 20 to 200 individuals, each of whom we knew at least in passing (Workman & Reader, 2021), we had no choice but to cooperate with one another in order to succeed both individually and as a group. Nowadays, this is also no longer the case, similar to the previous example regarding anxiety. We do not rely on other people as much for our own success in terms of survival. Someone living in New York City, for instance, is one of over eight million individuals. With that large a population there is no way to form altruistic relationships with everyone you encounter, not even in one's own neighborhood. Neighborhoods have shown to display significant indicators of a sense of community (see O'Brien & Wilson, 2011; O'Brien et al., 2014; Wilson, 2011) in various literatures. Therefore, when the size of our neighborhoods is too large (over 200 people), our sense of community may decrease. One city block alone may house well over 200 individuals. Since helping our neighbors and receiving help in return enhances one's emotional state (Underwood et al., 1977), when we do not have these connections with our neighbors our psychological health may suffer.

Our modern communities are a clear mismatch from those of our ancestors, but we can implement positive evolutionary psychological interventions to lessen said mismatch. Humans can form smaller communities within our larger ones, such as religious affiliations and other groups that facilitate bringing people together. Such examples may be found in small nonprofit organizations, bowling leagues, scout troops, and other small-scale groups that exist within larger social spheres. It is important for our mental well-being to find a sense of community, no matter how big or small of a city or town one resides in.

10.4 Workplace

Given how much time so many of us spend at work, understanding applications of positive evolutionary psychology in the workplace is similarly critical. For instance, the mismatch hypothesis may also account for poorer health and productivity among employees in their workplace (Nicholson, 2000). Incorporating principles of positive evolutionary psychology in the workplace can help to decrease this mismatch, hence increasing employees' physical as well as psychological well-being. Research has found that integrating elements similar to those of the environment of evolutionary adaptedness in the workplace produces beneficial effects. Some have argued that humans' early life in the savanna may be the reason for *biophilia* – the human inclination to be around nature (Hinds & Sparks, 2011; Wilson, 1984). Our psychological well-being can be enhanced through exposure to nature, notably sunlight (Holick, 2004) and greenery (Dingle et al., 2000). Additionally, natural behaviors such as social interactions (Repetti, 1993) and physical movement (Lechner et al., 1997) have also been shown to have benefits in the workplace. One can try putting a plant on their desk, taking short walks around the office throughout the day, or speaking more often with coworkers in order to improve life satisfaction.

10.5 Physical Health

As described in See section 9, a final major issue to highlight in terms of takeaways related to positive evolutionary psychology bears on the nature of physical health and evolutionary mismatch. Earlier in this Element, we discussed how our ancestors engaged in physical exercise on a much higher frequency than we do today, which has detrimental effects on modern human's health. Positive evolutionary psychology may serve as an intervention in helping us boost our levels of activity and thus living more similarly to our ancestors. Realistically, one will not be walking twenty miles per day, as humans did in the environment of evolutionary adaptedness (see Geher & Wedberg, 2020; Wolf, 2010), but try setting a more reachable goal. Perhaps one may substitute driving to the drugstore for walking there or find a gym buddy to help motivate them on those days when a workout just does not seem possible. These may seem like slight changes, or they may seem large, depending on the lifestyle one currently lives; but any improvement, no matter how big or small, will be beneficial to one's physical health. Changes in diet and exercise can aid in living a more fulfilled life.

11 Bottom Line

The human experience is complex, to understate the case. Positive psychology has demonstrated to be a very powerful scientific approach to help us understand factors that facilitate positive growth at the individual and community levels (see Peterson, 2013). This said, it is clear that positive psychologists have, to this point, largely ignored the evolutionary perspective (see Geher & Wedberg, 2020). This fact is concerning given how powerful Darwin's ideas are in shedding light on the entirety of the human experience (see Carmen et al., 2013).

Using principles such as *behavioral adaptations, evolutionary mismatch, reciprocal altruism,* and *Dunbar's number,* the evolutionary approach to understanding the human experience dovetails extraordinarily with the content of positive psychology. Positive evolutionary psychology is an attempt to integrate these two paradigms in a way that helps advance the goals of positive psychology by using behavioral science to make improvements to the human condition at the individual and community levels, employing the most powerful ideas that have ever existed in the life sciences: Darwin's ideas on evolution.

Importantly, in many ways, the idea of positive evolutionary psychology can be thought of as an integration of several critical lines of scholarship in the behavioral sciences writ large. In recent years, such intellectual powerhouses as Douglas Kenrick (Kenrick & Lundberg-Kenrick, 2022) and Scott Barry Kaufman (Kaufman, 2020) have researched extensively how various threads of empirical research in the behavioral sciences, much of which is rooted in evolutionary principles, shed light on such positive psychological goals as finding meaning in life, cultivating positive emotions, and cultivating prosocial and well-functioning communities. Similarly, scholars such as Nesse and Williams (1995) and Shiota et al. (2017) have used evolutionary principles to help elucidate issues of human emotions, which sit largely near the core of positive evolutionary psychology. Similarly, evolutionary biologist David Sloan Wilson (2019) has famously worked to utilize evolutionary approaches to understanding human sociality in ways that can be applied to positive growth at both the individual and group, or community, levels. In integrating these research traditions under the umbrella term of positive evolutionary psychology, we seek to provide a singular and clear framework for understanding how evolutionary principles, across the entirety of the field of evolutionary studies, can be used to push the needle of the human experience in positive ways.

We hope that this Element provides a guide for how to apply Darwin's ideas to important issues of the human condition, including such large-scale institutions as educational systems, political systems, and religious institutions, along with more proximate psychological issues at the individual and dyadic levels such as the building of trusting relationships and the attainment of genuine growth, meaning, and happiness in life. Here is to the use of Darwin's ideas to make the world a better place. Here is to positive evolutionary psychology!

References

Allen-Arave, W., Gurven, M., & Hill, K. (2008). Reciprocal altruism, rather than kin selection, maintains nepotistic food transfers on an Ache reservation. *Evolution and Human Behavior*, *29*(5), 305–318. https://doi.org/10.1016/j.evolhumbehav.2008.03.002.

Barrett-Cheetham, E., Williams, L. A., & Bednall, T. C. (2016). A differentiated approach to the link between positive emotion, motivation, and eudaimonic well-being. *The Journal of Positive Psychology*, *11*(6), 595–608. https://doi.org/10.1080/17439760.2016.1152502.

Bildhauer, B. (2013). Medieval European conceptions of blood: Truth and human integrity. *Journal of the Royal Anthropology Institute*, *19*, 57–76. https://doi.org/10.1111/1467-9655.12016.

Bingham, P. M., & Souza, J. (2009). *Death from a distance and the birth of a humane universe*. BookSurge.

Bjorklund, D. F. (2021). *How children invented humanity: The role of development in human evolution*. Oxford University Press.

Bjorklund, D.F. (2022). Children's Evolved Learning Abilities and Their Implications for Education. *Educational Psychology Review*, 34, 2243–2273. https://doi.org/10.1007/s10648-022-09688-z

Bjorklund, D. F. (2023). *Children's thinking: Cognitive development and individual differences* (7th ed.). Sage.

Boiler, L., Haverman, M., Westerhof, G. J. et al. (2013). Positive psychology interventions: A meta-analysis of randomized controlled studies. *BMC Public Health*, *13*, 119. https://doi.org/10.1186/1471-2458-13-119.

Bowlby, J. (1969). *Attachment and loss*. Basic Books.

Bugental, J. F. T. (1964). The third force in psychology. *Journal of Humanistic Psychology*, *4*(1), 19–26.

Burnham T. C. (2016). Economics and evolutionary mismatch: Humans in novel settings do not maximize. *Journal of Bioeconomics*, *18*, 195–209. https://doi.org/10.1007/s10818-016-9233-8.

Buss, D. M. (2019). *Evolutionary psychology: The new science of the mind*. Routledge.

Buss, D. M. (2000). The evolution of happiness. *American Psychologist*, *55*, 15–23. https://doi.org/10.1037/0003-066x.55.1.15.

Carmen, R. A., Geher, G., Glass, D. J. et al. (2013). Evolution integrated across all islands of the human behavioral archipelago: All psychology as evolutionary psychology. *EvoS Journal: The Journal of the Evolutionary Studies Consortium*, *5*(1), 108–126.

Carver, C. S., Sinclair, S., & Johnson, S. L. (2010). Authentic and hubristic pride: Differential relations to aspects of goal regulation, affect, and self-control. *Journal of Research in Personality*, *44*, 698–703. https://doi .org/10.1016/j.jrp.2010.09.004.

Colegrave N. (2012). The evolutionary success of sex: Science & society series on sex and science. *EMBO Reports 13*(9), 774–778. https://doi.org/10.1038/ embor.2012.109.

Confer, J. C., Easton, J. A., Fleischman, D. S. et al. (2010). Evolutionary psychology: Controversies, questions, prospects, and limitations. *American Psychologist*, *65*(2), 110–126. https://doi.org/10.1037/a0018413.

Cordain, L., Eaton, S. B., Sebastian, A. et al. (2005). Origins and evolution of the western diet: Health implications for the 21st century. *American Society for Nutrition*, *81*(*2*), 341–354. https://doi.org/10.1093/ajcn.81.2.341.

Cosmides, L., & Tooby, J. (1992). Cognitive adaptations for social exchange. In J. H. Barkow, L. Cosmides, & J. Tooby (Eds.), *The adapted mind: Evolutionary psychology and the generation of culture* (pp. 163–228). Oxford University Press.

Daly, M., & Wilson, M. I. (1997). Crime and conflict: homicide in evolutionary psychological perspective. *Crime and Justice*, *22*, 251–300. https://doi.org/ 10.1086/449260.

Darwin, C. (1872). *The expression of the emotions in man and animals*. John Murray. https://doi.org/10.1037/10001-000.

De'Jesús, A. R., Cristo, M., Ruel, M. et al. (2021). Betrayal, outrage, guilt, and forgiveness: The four horsemen of the human social-emotional experience. *The Journal of the Evolutionary Studies Consortium*, *9*(1), 1–13.

de Waal, F. B. M. (2002). Primates – A natural heritage of conflict resolution. *Science*, *289*, 586–590. https://doi.org/10.1126/science.289.5479.586.

Dingle, P., Tapsell, P., & Hu, S. (2000). Reducing formaldehyde exposure in office environments using plants. *Bulletin of Environmental Contamination and Toxicology*, *64*, 302–308. https://doi.org/10.1007/s001289910044.

Diraddo, D. (2022). 15 surprising facts and statistics about the fast food industry. Toast. https://pos.toasttab.com/blog/on-the-line/fast-food-industry-statistics, January 2, 2023

Dunbar, R. I. M. (1992). Neocortex size as a constraint on group size in primates. *Journal of Human Evolution*, *22*(6), 469–493. https://doi.org/ 10.1016/0047-2484(92)90081-j.

Dunbar, R. I. M. (1998). The social brain hypothesis. *Evolutionary Anthropology*, *6*, 178–190. https://doi.org/10.1002/(sici)1520-6505(1998) 6:5%3C178::aid-evan5%3E3.0.co;2-8.

Eberhard, M. J. W. (1975). The evolution of social behavior by kin selection. *The Quarterly Review of Biology, 50*, 1–33.

Fell, J., & Geher, G. (2018). Psychological outcomes associated with crossfit. *Journal of Evolution and Health, 2*(2), Article 7. https://doi.org/10.15310/2334-3591.1071.

Figueredo, A. J., Vásquez, G., Brumbach, B. H., & Schneider, S. M. R. (2006). The heritability of life history strategy: The k-factor, covitality, and personality. *Biodemography and Social Biology, 51*, 121–143. https://doi.org/10.1080/19485565.2004.9989090.

Flaherty, S. C., & Sadler L. S. (2011). A review of attachment theory in the context of adolescent parenting. *Journal of Pediatric Health Care, 25*, 114–121. https://doi.org/10.1016/j.pedhc.2010.02.005.

Flinn, M. V., Quinlan, R. J., Decker, S. A., Turner, M. T., & England, B. G. (1996). Male-female differences in effects of parental absence on glucocorticoid stress response. *Human Nature, 7*(2), 125–162. https://doi.org/10.1007/BF02692108.

Flinn, M. V., Quinlan, R. J., Coe, K., & Ward, C. V. (2007). Evolution of the human family: Cooperative males, long social childhoods, smart mothers, and extended kin networks. In C. A. Salmon & T. K. Shackelford (Eds.), *Family relationships: An evolutionary perspective* (pp. 16–38). Oxford University Press. https://doi.org/10.1093/acprof:oso/9780195320510.003.0002.

Gable, S. L. & Haidt, J. (2005). What (and why) is positive psychology? *Review of General Psychology, 9*(2), 103–110. https://doi.org/10.1037/1089-2680.9.2.103.

Geary, D. C. (2005). Evolution of paternal investment. In D. M. Buss (ed.), *Handbook of evolutionary psychology* (pp. 483–505). John Wiley & Sons.

Geary, D. C., & Berch, D. B. (2016). Evolution and children's cognitive and academic development. In D. C. Geary & D. B. Berch (eds.), *Evolutionary perspectives on education and child development* (pp. 217–250). Springer.

Geher, G. (2011). Evolutionarily informed parenting: A ripe area for scholarship in evolutionary studies. *EvoS Journal: The Journal of the Evolutionary Studies Consortium, 3*(2), 26–36.

Geher, G. (2014). *Evolutionary psychology 101*. Springer.

Geher, G. Di Santo, J. M., Planke, J. et al. (2020). Dark parenting: Parents who score as high in the dark triad demonstrate non-authoritative parenting styles. *EvoS Journal: The Journal of the Evolutionary Studies Consortium, 11*(1), 116–143.

Geher, G., Carmen, R., Guitar, A. et al. (2015). The evolutionary psychology of small-scale versus large-scale politics: Ancestral conditions did not include large-scale politics. *European Journal of Social Psychology, 46*(3), 369–376. https://doi.org/10.1002/ejsp.2158.

Geher, G., & Gambacorta, D. (2010). Evolution is not relevant to sex differences in humans because I want it that way! *EvoS Journal: The Journal of the Evolutionary Studies Consortium, 2*(1), 32–47.

Geher, G., & Wedberg, N. (2020). *Positive evolutionary psychology: Darwin's guide to living a richer life*. Oxford University Press.

Gray, P. (2011). The special value of age-mixed play. *American Journal of Play, 3*, 500–522.

Gray, P. (2020). How children coped in the first months of the pandemic lockdown: Free time, play, family togetherness, and helping out at home. *American Journal of Play, 13*, 33–52.

Grinde, B. (2002). Happiness in the perspective of evolutionary psychology. *Journal of Happiness Studies, 3*(4), 331–354.

Gruskin, K., & Geher, G. (2018). The evolved classroom: Using evolutionary theory to inform elementary pedagogy. *Evolutionary Behavioral Sciences, 12*(4), 336–347. https://doi.org/10.1037/ebs0000111.

Guitar, A, E., Glass, D. J., Geher, G., & Suvak, M. K. (2018). Situation-specific emotional states: Testing Nesse and Ellsworth's (2009) model of emotions for situations that arise in goal pursuit using virtual-world software. *Current Psychology* 39, 1245–1259. https://doi.org/10.1007/s12144-018-9830-x.

Haidt, J. (2003). The moral emotions. In R. J. Davidson, K. R. Scherer, & H. H. Goldsmith (eds.), Handbook of affective sciences (pp. 852–870). Oxford University Press.

Hamilton, W. D. (1964). The genetical evolution of social behavior. I. *Journal of Theoretical Biology, 7*, 1–16. https://doi.org/10.1016/0022-5193(64)90038-4.

Hawkes, K., O'Connell, J. F., Jones, N. G. B., Alvarez, H., & Charnov, E. L. (1998). Grandmothering, menopause, and the evolution of human life histories. *Proceedings of the National Academy of Sciences, 95*(3), 1336–1339. https://doi.org/10.1073/pnas.95.3.1336.

Henrich, J., Boyd, R., & Richerson, P. J. (2012). The puzzle of monogamous marriage. *Philosophical Transactions of the Royal Society B: Biological Sciences, 367*(1589), 657–669. https://doi.org/10.1098/rstb.2011.0290.

Henrich, J., & Gil-White, F. J. (2001). The evolution of prestige: Freely conferred deference as a mechanism for enhancing the benefits of cultural transmission. *Evolution and Human Behavior, 22*(3), 165–196. https://doi.org/10.1016/s1090-5138(00)00071-4.

Hill, K., & Hurtado, A. M. (1996). *Aché life history: The ecology and demography of a foraging people.* Aldine de Gruyter.

Hinds, J., & Sparks, P. (2011). The affective quality of human-natural environment relationships. *Evolutionary Psychology, 9*, 451–469. https://doi.org/10.1177/147470491100900314.

Holick, M. F. (2004). Vitamin D is important in the prevention of cancers, type 1 diabetes, heart disease, and osteoporosis. *American Journal of Clinical Nutrition, 79*, 362–371. https://doi.org/10.1097/01.smj.0000140865.32054.db.

Hrdy, S. B. (2009). *Mothers and others: The evolutionary origins of mutual understanding.* Harvard University Press.

Kanazawa S. (2004). The savanna principle. *Managerial and Decision Economics, 25*, 41–54. https://doi.org/10.1002/mde.1130.

Kaplan H. S., Lancaster J. B., Anderson K. G. (1998). Human parental investment and fertility: The life histories of men in Albuquerque. In A. Booth & A. C. Crouter (eds.), *Men in families: When do they get involved? What difference does it make?* (pp. 55–109). Erlbaum.

Kaufman, S. B. (2020). *Transcend: The new science of self-actualization.* TarcherPerigree.

Kenrick, D. T., Griskevicius, V., Neuberg, S. L., & Schaller, M. (2010). Renovating the pyramid of needs: Contemporary extensions built upon ancient foundations. *Perspectives on Psychological Science, 5*, 292–314. https://doi.org/10.1177/1745691610369469.

Kenrick, D. T., & Lundberg-Kenrick, D. E. (2022). *Solving modern problems with a stone-age brain: Human evolution and the seven fundamental motives.* American Psychological Association. https://doi.org/10.1037/0000286-000

Khazaei, F., Khazaei, O., & Ghanbari-H, B. (2017). Positive psychology interventions for Internet addiction treatment. *Computers in Human Behavior, 72*, 304–311. https://doi.org/10.1016/j.chb.2017.02.065.

Ko, A., Pick, C. M., Kwon, J. Y. et al. (2020). Family values: Rethinking the psychology of human social motivation. *Perspectives on Psychological Science, 15* (1), 173–201. https://doi.org/10.31234/osf.io/u8h3x.

Krettenauer, T., Jia, F., & Mosleh, M. (2011). The role of emotion expectancies in adolescents' moral decision making. *Journal of Experimental Child Psychology, 108*(2), 358–370. https://doi.org/10.1016/j.jecp.2010.08.014.

Lechner, L., DeVries, H., Adriaansen, S., & Drabbels, L. (1997). Effects of an employee fitness program on reduced absenteeism. *Journal of Occupational and Environmental Medicine, 38*, 827–883. https://doi.org/10.1097/00043764-199709000-00005.

Leontopoulou, S. (2015). A positive psychology intervention with emerging adults. *The European Journal of Counseling Psychology, 3*(2), 113–116. https://doi.org/10.5964/ejcop.v3i2.33.

Li, N. P., van Vugt, M., & Colarelli, S. M. (2018). The evolutionary mismatch hypothesis: Implications for psychological science. *Current Directions in Psychological Science, 27*(1), 38–44. https://doi.org/10.1177/0963721 417731378.

LoBue, V., & Adolph, K. E. (2019). Fear in infancy: Lessons from snakes, spiders, heights, and strangers. *Developmental Psychology, 55*(9), 1889–1907. https://doi.org/10.1037/dev0000675.

Mace, R. (2015). The evolutionary ecology of the family. In D. M. Buss (ed.), *Handbook of evolutionary psychology* (pp. 483–505). John Wiley & Sons. https://doi.org/10.1002/9781119125563.evpsych122.

Maner J. K., & Kenrick D. T. (2010). When adaptations go awry: Functional and dysfunctional aspects of social anxiety. *Social Issues and Policy Review, 4*, 111–142. https://doi.org/10.1111/j.1751-2409.2010.01019.x.

Maslow, A. H. (1943). A theory of human motivation. *Psychological Review, 50*, 370–396. https://doi.org/10.1037/h0054346.

Mauro, R., Sato, K., & Tucker, J. (1992). The role of appraisal in human emotions: A cross-cultural study. *Journal of Personality and Social Psychology, 62*(2), 301–317. https://doi.org/10.1037/0022-3514.62.2.301.

McCauley, T. G., Bilingsley J., & McCullough, M. E. (2022). An evolutionary psychology view of forgiveness: Individuals, groups, and culture. *Current Opinion in Psychology, 44*, 275–280. https://doi.org/10.31234/osf.io/c4f2k.

McMahan, E. A., & Estes, D. (2015). The effect of contact with natural environments on positive and negative affect: A meta-analysis. *The Journal of Positive Psychology, 10*, 507–519, https://doi.org/10.1080/17439760.2014.994224.

Michie, S. (2009). Pride and gratitude: How positive emotions influence the prosocial behaviors of organizational leaders. *Journal of Leadership & Organizational Studies, 15*, 393–403. https://doi.org/10.1177/1548051 809333338.

Miller, G. F. (2000). *The mating mind: How sexual choice shaped the evolution of human nature*. Doubleday.

Nakamura, J. (2013). Pride and the experience of meaning in daily life. *The Journal of Positive Psychology, 8*(6), 555–567. https://doi.org/10.1080/ 17439760.2013.830765.

National Alliance on Mental Illness. (2022, June). *Mental Health by the Numbers* Retrieved August, 2022 from www.nami.org/mhstats.

Nesse, R. M., & Williams, G. C. (1995). *Why we get sick: The new science of Darwinian medicine.* Vintage Books.

Nesse, R. M., & Ellsworth, P. C. (2009). *Evolution, emotions, and emotional disorders. American Psychologist, 64*(2), 129–139. https://doi.org/10.1037/a0013503.

Nicholson, N. (2000). *Managing the human animal: Why people behave the way they do in corporate settings.* Texere.

O'Brien, D. T., & Wilson, D. S. (2011). Community Perception: The ability to assess the safety of unfamiliar neighborhoods and respond adaptively. *Journal of Personality and Social Psychology, 100*, 606–620. https://doi.org/10.1037/a0022803.

O'Brien, D. T., Gordon, E., & Phillipi-Baldwin, J. (2014). Territoriality, attachment to space and community, and maintenance of the public space: A field study integrating administrative records of reports of public issues with self-reports. *Journal of Environmental Psychology, 40*, 320–330.

Öhman, A., & Mineka, S. (2001). *Fears, phobias, and preparedness: Toward an evolved module of fear and fear learning. Psychological Review, 108*, 483–522. https://doi.org/10.1037/0033-295x.108.3.483.

Pavard, S., Koons, D. N., & Heyer, E. (2007). The influence of maternal care in shaping human survival and fertility. *Evolution, 61*(12), 2801–2810. doi:10.1111/j.1558-5646.2007.00236.x.

Peterson, C. (2013). *Pursuing the good life: 100 reflections on positive psychology.* Oxford University Press.

Pinker, S. (2012). *The better angels of our nature.* Penguin.

Pinker, S. (1994). *The language instinct.* William Morrow.

Platek, S., Geher, G., Heywood, L. et al. (2011). Walking the walk to teach the talk: Implementing ancestral lifestyle changes as the newest tool in evolutionary studies. *Evolution: Education & Outreach, 4*, 41–51. https://doi.org/10.1007/s12052-010-0309-y.

Profet, M. (1997). Pregnancy sickness: Using your body's natural defenses to protect your baby-to-be. Hachette Books.

Repetti, R. L. (1993). Short-term effects of occupational stressors on daily mood and health complaints. *Health Psychology, 12*, 125–131. https://doi.org/10.1037/0278-6133.12.2.125.

Ruff, C. (2002). Variation in human body size and shape. *Annual Review of Anthropology, 31*(1), 211–232. https://doi.org/10.1146/annurev.anthro.31.040402.085407.

Schueller, S. M., & Parks, A. C. (2014). The science of self-help: Translating positive psychology research into increased individual happiness. *European Psychologist*, *19*(2), 145–155. https://doi.org/10.1027/1016-9040/a000181.

Schlaepfer M. A., Runge M. C., & Sherman P. W. (2002). Ecological and evolutionary traps. *Trends in Ecology & Evolution*, *17*, 474–480. https://doi.org/10.1016/s0169-5347(02)02580-6.

Seligman, M. E. P., & Csikszentmihalyi, M. (2000). Positive psychology: An introduction. *American Psychologist*, *55*(1), 5–14. https://doi.org/10.1037/0003-066X.55.1.5.

Sergeant, S., & Mongrain, M. (2015). Distressed users report a better response to online positive psychology interventions than nondistressed users. *Canadian Psychology / Psychologie Canadienne*, *56*(3), 322–331. https://doi.org/10.1037/cap0000034.

Shiota, M. N., Campos, B., Oveis, C. et al. (2017). *Beyond happiness: Building a science of discrete positive emotions. American Psychologist*, *72*(7), 617–643. https://doi.org/10.1037/a0040456.

Sin, N. L., & Lyubomirsky, S. (2009). Enhancing well-being and alleviating depressive symptoms with positive psychology interventions: a practice-friendly meta-analysis. *Journal of Clinical Psychology*, *65*(5), 467–487. https://doi.org/10.1002/jclp.20593.

Spranger J. A., Colarelli S. M., Dimotakis N., Jacob A., & Arvey R. D. (2012). Effects of kin density within family-owned businesses. *Organizational Behavior and Human Decision Processes*, *119*, 151–162. https://doi.org/10.1016/j.obhdp.2012.07.001.

Srivastava, K. (2009). Urbanization and mental health. *Industrial Psychiatry Journal*, *18*, 75–76. https://doi.org/10.4103/0972-6748.64028.

Sznycer, D., Al-Shawaf, L., Bereby-Meyer, Y. et al. (2017). Cross-cultural regularities in the cognitive architecture of pride. *Proceedings of the National Academy of Sciences*, *114*(8),1874–1879. https://doi.org/10.1073/pnas.1614389114.

Sznycer, D., Xygalatas, D., Alami, S. et al. (2018). Invariances in the architecture of pride across small-scale societies. *Proceedings of the National Academy of Sciences*, *115*(33), 8322–8327. https://doi.org/10.1073/pnas.1808418115.

Symons, D. (1979). *The evolution of human sexuality.* Oxford University Press.

Tinbergen, N. (1953). *The herring gull's world.* Collins.

Tomasello, M. (2019). *Becoming human: A theory of Ontogeny.* Belknap Press.

Tooby J., & Cosmides L. (1990). The past explains the present: Emotional adaptations and the structure of ancestral environments. *Ethology and Sociobiology, 11*, 375–424. https://doi.org/10.1016/0162-3095(90)90017-z.

Tracy, J. L., Cheng, J. T., Robins, R. W., & Trzesniewski, K. H. (2009). Authentic and hubristic pride: The affective core of self-esteem and Narcissism. *Self and Identity, 8*, 196–213. https://doi.org/10.1080/15298860802505053.

Trivers, R. L. (1971). The evolution of reciprocal altruism. *The Quarterly Review of Biology, 46*, 35–37. https://doi.org/10.1086/406755.

Trivers, R. L. (1972). Parental investment and sexual selection. In B. Campbell (ed.), *Sexual selection and the descent of man*: 1871–1971 (pp. 136–179). Aldine. https://doi.org/10.4324/9781315129266-7.

Twenge, J. M. (2017). iGen: Why Today's Super-Connected Kids Are Growing Up Less Rebellious, More Tolerant, Less Happy and Completely Unprepared for Adulthood. Atria.

Underwood, B., Froming, W. J., & Moore, B. S. (1977). Mood, attention, and altruism: A search for mediating variables. *Developmental Psychology, 13*, 541–542. https://doi.org/10.1037/0012-1649.13.5.541.

van Vugt M., & Ronay R. D. (2014). The evolutionary psychology of leadership: Theory, review, and roadmap. *Organizational Psychology Review, 4*, 74–95. https://doi.org/10.1177/2041386613493635.

Verbeke, W., Belschak, F., & Bagozzi, R. P. (2004). The adaptive consequences of pride in personal selling. *Journal of the Academy of Marketing Science, 32*, 386–402. https://doi.org/10.1177/0092070304267105.

Watkins, P. (2014). *Positive psychology 101*. Springer.

Williams L. A., & DeSteno D. (2008). Pride and perseverance: The motivational role of pride. *Journal of Personality and Social Psychology, 94*, 1007–1017. https://doi.org/10.1037/0022-3514.94.6.1007.

Wilson, D. S. (2007). *Evolution for everyone: How Darwin's theory can change the way we think about our lives*. Delacorte Press.

Wilson, D. S. (2011). *The Neighborhood Project: Using evolution to improve my city, one block at a time*. Little, Brown.

Wilson, D. S. (2019). *This View of Life: Completing the Darwinian revolution*. Pantheon.

Wilson, E. O. (1984). *Biophilia*. Harvard University Press.

Wolf, R. (2010). *The paleo solution*. Victory Belt.

Workman, L., & Reader, W. (2021). *Evolutionary psychology: An introduction*. Cambridge University Press.

Zimbardo, P. G. (2007). *The Lucifer effect: Understanding how good people turn evil*. Random House.

Author Note

Except for the first author, all authors contributed equally and their names in the order are based alphabetically. We have no conflicts of interest to disclose.

Cambridge Elements $\equiv$

Applied Evolutionary Science

David F. Bjorklund
Florida Atlantic University

David F. Bjorklund is a Professor of Psychology at Florida Atlantic University in Boca Raton, Florida. He is the Editor-in-Chief of the *Journal of Experimental Child Psychology*, the Vice President of the Evolution Institute, and has written numerous articles and books on evolutionary developmental psychology, with a particular interest in the role of immaturity in evolution and development.

About the Series
This series presents original, concise, and authoritative reviews of key topics in applied evolutionary science. Highlighting how an evolutionary approach can be applied to real-world social issues, many Elements in this series will include findings from programs that have produced positive educational, social, economic, or behavioral benefits. Cambridge Elements in Applied Evolutionary Science is published in association with the Evolution Institute.

 THE EVOLUTION INSTITUTE

Cambridge Elements $\equiv$

Applied Evolutionary Science

Elements in the Series

Improving Breastfeeding Rates: Evolutionary Anthropological Insights for Public Health
Emily H. Emmott

The Hidden Talents Framework: Implications for Science, Policy, and Practice
Bruce J. Ellis, Laura S. Abrams, Ann S. Masten, Robert J. Sternberg, Nim Tottenham and Willem E. Frankenhuis

An Introduction to Positive Evolutionary Psychology
Glenn Geher, Megan Fritche, Avrey Goodwine, Julia Lombard, Kaitlyn Longo and Darcy Montana

A full series listing is available at: www.cambridge.org/EAES

Printed in the United States
by Baker & Taylor Publisher Services